BECOME THE GLOBAL INDIAN

THE 9 ESSENTIAL SKILLS TO WORK WITH THE WEST

Lars Kåre Helgesen

ISBN
Paperback 979-8-89588-922-0
Hardcase 979-8-89699-413-8

Dedication

This book is dedicated to **my grandpa Kåre,** *whose encouragement from an early age continues to push me forward. Even though he's no longer here, he remains my greatest supporter, always present in the back of my mind.*

To my **girlfriend, Serine,** *who patiently listens to my endless stream of thoughts, ideas, and sometimes wild activities—thank you for standing by me and always supporting my ambitions.*

To my **parents, Svanhild** *and* **Rolf,** *who have been my rock through every challenge and triumph. Your love and constant support have made everything possible.*

Lastly, a thank you to my **Indian friends, Joseph** *and* **Vatsal,** *for always being there to answer my questions and clarifications, no matter the time of day. Your wisdom and willingness to engage have been invaluable throughout this journey.*

Take the First Step to Mastery

Welcome to *Become the Global Indian*! By opening this book, you've already taken a bold step toward mastering the skills you need to thrive in Western business environments. But why stop here? Accelerate your growth and make the most of your journey with the full Global Indian course at **www.larshelgesen.com** and join the Global Indian Community.

Here's what you'll unlock:

- **Exclusive Videos:** Join me as I bring each skill to life with actionable tips and relatable examples.
- **Engaging Animations:** Grasp concepts quickly and remember them effortlessly.
- **Scenario-Based Quizzes:** Test your knowledge with real-world challenges and refine your approach.
- **Official Certification:** Highlight your expertise and position yourself as a standout Global Indian.
- **Free Cheat Sheet:** Keep the 9 essential skills at your fingertips—your perfect go-to guide.
- **And more:** Gain access to bonus tools, expert resources, and ongoing guidance for your success.

As a reader of this book, you're already part of the Global Indian community. Use the code **TGI2025** to receive 10% off the course price.

Your journey starts now. Visit **www.larshelgesen.com** and begin mastering the skills that will take you to new heights.

Contents

Prologue

The Beginning of a Journey

❧✳❧

Here I sit, writing the first words of this book. It's a winter evening in Norway, and I've just missed my train. I had planned to return to Oslo, the capital of Norway where I live, after spending a few days with my family in the mountains. The evening started simply—I was in my dad's car, discussing the features of his new Volvo. When the train arrived, I rushed out, hugged my dad goodbye, and found my seat on the train.

Settling in, I was struck by the difference between this moment and my past travels in India. In Norway, I had an entire section to myself, a luxury unimaginable in India, where one might share a berth with a complete stranger. Lost in a book, I heard 'Geilo' announced over the speakers. My pulse quickened—Geilo wasn't part of my route. That's when I realized I had boarded a train heading in the wrong direction.

Instead of panicking, I chose to embrace the unexpected. I decided to get off at Voss and wait for the night train back to Oslo. And so, here I am, at a bar in the Scandic Hotel in Voss, with a beer by my side, writing the first words of this book. The tension from missing the train has faded, replaced by a sense of calm acceptance. The Red Hot Chili Peppers play softly over the speakers, and as I sit here, I reflect on life's twists and turns—moments we don't see coming but that shape us all the same.

Much like this moment, my life took an unexpected turn when I was told I'd be heading to India. It's a twist that changed everything and brought me to the heart of this book.

In March 2023, I was sent to India by my employer with a clear objective: understand how to improve the collaboration between our teams. We had been working with India for over a decade, but the partnership had never quite clicked. I was the third person sent to figure out why, and I would spend the next six months living in Mumbai, working to bridge that gap.

For me, this was more than just a professional mission—it was the adventure I had been waiting for. The months leading up to the trip were filled with preparation. I read books about India, watched Bollywood films, and curated playlists featuring Indian music. But what fascinated me most, even before arriving, were the people.

People have always intrigued me—how we think, how our surroundings shape us, and how, despite our differences, we are fundamentally alike. I've always been curious about how culture molds us, and India, with its rich diversity, became the perfect lens through which to explore this.

This book, however, is not an attempt to teach you about your own culture. You know that already. Instead, it's about recognizing that no cultures are the same. It's about giving you a glimpse into **how we in the West work and interact,** so that we can collaborate better. There are books written to explain Indian culture to the West, but none that explain Western culture to Indians. This book aims to fill that gap.

Why I Wrote This Book

India is one of the world's largest economies, and millions of Indians play vital roles in global business, supporting companies across sectors. This book is intended to raise awareness of how work and collaboration are approached in the West. While it's impossible to change a culture that has developed over centuries, we can all increase our awareness of other cultures and adapt where necessary to ensure success in today's interconnected world.

The first step in adapting to another culture is understanding your own. I hope this book helps you reflect on your own cultural norms and think deeply about how things really are. If you embrace the framework laid out here, I'm confident you will find success in navigating cultural differences, whether working directly with Western colleagues or interacting with Western clients.

My First Meeting with India

I still remember that cold March night in Norway. I was heading to India, and my mind was racing. As I boarded the plane, I had no idea that the journey ahead would shape not only my career but the very foundation of this book.

India greeted me with a sensory overload—vibrant colors, bustling roads, and the warm, humid air of Mumbai. As I stood at the airport, soaking it all in, I quickly realized that I was entering a world completely different from the one I had left behind in Norway. This was the moment that sparked a journey of understanding, one that led me to write this book.

During my six months in India, I observed firsthand the **cultural contrasts** that affected not just social interactions, but the way we worked, communicated, and approached collaboration. It became clear to me that understanding these differences wasn't just helpful—it was **essential** for success.

Introduction

The Global Advantage

ತಿ❋ರ

The knowledge you didn't realize you needed is what will unlock the doors to success in the Western workplace.

The Cultural Gap

My first encounter with an Indian colleague, Priya, happened a few months into my career as an M&A consultant at one of the big four consultancy firms. It was 2020, and Priya had been assigned to help me with an Excel Databook. We worked remotely, communicating mostly through emails. To me, the tasks seemed simple—nothing that should pose a problem for someone with five years of experience. But what followed was surprising.

Priya repeatedly asked for confirmation on basic tasks, seeking approval for every step. In our virtual meetings, she was incredibly reserved, almost too quiet to hear, and her camera quality didn't help. The work she delivered had errors, and it felt like she lacked the confidence or independence I expected. Frustrated, I eventually had to redo much of the work myself. I remember thinking, *How could someone with five years of experience struggle like this?*

I gave her poor feedback, assuming the problem was a lack of skills or self-sufficiency. At the time, it didn't occur to me that there could be something else at play—something much deeper than technical competence.

Fast forward three years, and I found myself in Mumbai, meeting Priya face-to-face for the first time. What I encountered was a completely different person—open, confident, and full of energy. Among her colleagues, she was lively, laughing, and engaging in a way I hadn't seen in our virtual interactions. It was then that I began to realize: the issues we faced during our initial collaboration were not about her capabilities. They were about **cultural differences.**

The reserved and deferential way Priya communicated wasn't a sign of insecurity or incompetence—it was how she had been taught to approach work in her cultural context. The Western work environment, which prizes assertiveness and independence, was unfamiliar territory for her. What I had interpreted as hesitancy was, in fact, an effort to respect hierarchy by giving me the respect she thought I wanted, though that was not the case.

This realization marked the beginning of my journey toward understanding the importance of cultural differences in the workplace, and ultimately, the reason for writing this book.

Why This Book Matters

Cultural gaps lie hidden—until they surface as challenges.

India is a rising global powerhouse. Its professionals are working in nearly every industry, supporting teams and companies in the U.S., Europe, Australia, and beyond. But the reality is, **mastering technical skills is no longer enough.** Success in today's global workforce requires understanding the **unspoken rules** that govern how business is done in Western cultures—rules that aren't always apparent to those coming from a different background.

This book is here to help you navigate that space, to give you the tools to **bridge the cultural divide** and succeed in a Western work environment while maintaining your own identity. Whether you're working remotely with Western colleagues, living abroad, or preparing for future global opportunities, the skills in this book will empower you to **thrive** where others struggle.

What I learned from working with Priya, and from years of experience collaborating with talented Indian professionals, is that **cultural gaps are often invisible until they create problems.** They don't manifest in obvious ways, but rather in subtle misunderstandings—missed promotions, feedback that doesn't land, and efforts that go unnoticed. It's not because Indian professionals aren't capable; it's because the **expectations and norms** in Western environments are different, and no one teaches you how to navigate them.

This Book Is About Changing That

It will show you how to recognize these differences, adapt when necessary, and turn cultural challenges into opportunities for growth. By mastering the skills in this book, you'll not only be able to **work more effectively across cultures.**

The Nine Essential Skills

Before we dive into the nine skills, it's essential to understand what they represent. These skills are not just about overcoming common challenges; **they are your roadmap to understanding, managing, and ultimately fulfilling the expectations that Western managers and clients will have of you.** Each skill is designed to help you adapt to the unspoken norms and values that drive success in Western workplaces. By mastering these skills, you'll align your work style with what Western professionals value—autonomy, efficiency, direct communication, and consistency. These are the keys to building trust, gaining recognition, and ensuring your long-term success in a global work environment.

You must come to terms with the fact that these skills challenge deeply ingrained Indian traditions, values, and norms—such as the emphasis on maintaining harmony, the hierarchical view of respect, and the belief that relationships are the cornerstone of both business and personal connections. To thrive, you must dare to embrace the unfamiliar and remain open to new perspectives that may redefine your approach.

Skill 1: Understand Why You Need to Adapt

Before anything else, you must understand *why* adaptation is necessary. This sets the foundation for all the other skills, showing how small changes can lead to big success.

Skill 2: Embrace Fast-Paced Relationship-Building

Western relationships often start with light-hearted small talk and quick rapport-building. Learn to engage early, even with people you don't know; no introduction needed to set the foundation for stronger connections later.

Skill 3: Master Clear, Honest Communication

Direct communication is key in the West. You'll discover how to be clear and transparent, talking without relying on body language or speaking around the context. This will help avoid misunderstandings and ensure your message is understood exactly as intended.

Skill 4: Value Time as a Precious Resource

Time is seen as limited in Western culture; they live by the phrase *"time is money."* You'll learn how to manage your time effectively and be seen as reliable.

Skill 5: Build Trust Through Consistency

Trust in the workplace isn't built overnight or through relationships. The foundation is delivering consistent, high-quality work – that's how you'll earn the trust and respect of your colleagues and superiors. One misunderstanding and trust might be broken.

Skill 6: Convince with Clear, Solution-Focused Arguments

In Western business environments, the ability to persuade with concise, solution-oriented arguments is highly valued. You'll learn how to present your ideas effectively.

Skill 7: Engage Directly with Superiors

In the West, hierarchy doesn't limit communication. Learn to engage confidently with your superiors and make your voice heard. Take initiative—don't wait for instructions. Be proactive, identify problems early, and propose solutions before anyone else even notices them.

Skill 8: Actively Participate in Discussions

Meetings in the West are collaborative. This skill will show you how to actively contribute, ensuring your voice shapes the conversation and that you aren't overlooked.

Skill 9: Present Yourself Professionally

Professionalism is about more than just doing the job—it's about how you present yourself, serving as the glue that holds all the skills together. Learn how to dress, speak, and show up in a way that will give you respect from a Western perspective.

Who This Book Is For

This book is primarily for Indian professionals navigating Western work environments or those aspiring to do so. Whether you're collaborating remotely with teams in the USA, Canada, or Europe or you plan to move to and work in a Western country, this guide is designed to help you succeed. You'll learn how to adapt to Western cultural norms while maintaining your own identity, giving you the skills to stand out in any professional setting.

But this book is not just about career advancement. It's also a roadmap for forming meaningful friendships and relationships with people from the West. Understanding how to build rapport and connect with Western colleagues on a personal level can be just as important as mastering workplace dynamics. If you've ever struggled to break through cultural barriers, whether at work or in social settings, the strategies in this book will give you the tools to form genuine, lasting connections.

Generalizations

Throughout this book, you'll notice references to both 'India' and 'The West' in broad, generalized terms. India is an incredibly diverse country, with vast differences in language, culture, and social norms across its regions. No single description can capture the full complexity of Indian society. However, this book focuses on common cultural patterns that frequently affect Indian professionals working in Western environments. While these patterns may not apply to every individual or situation, they provide valuable insights into the challenges many face when interacting with Western colleagues, as well as the difficulties Westerners experience when working with Indians.

Similarly, when I refer to 'The West,' I am speaking primarily about **Western Europe** (countries such as the U.K., Germany, France, Italy, the Netherlands, and Scandinavia) and **North America** (the U.S. and Canada), as well as **Australia** and **New Zealand**. While each of these regions has its own unique customs and workplace dynamics, they share several professional norms—such as direct communication or emphasis on punctuality - that tend to differ significantly from those in India.

I promise that all stories I share throughout this book are inspired by real stories, real companies, real people that I have met over the years. Though I have changed their names and details to maintain anonymity. However, culture is a sensitive topic, so keep in mind that this book is written by someone from the West; it's a Western view of the cultural barriers and struggles seen from our point of view. You might not agree with everything, you probably will not, but that's not the point, because you are now learning the struggles we face, which is the meaning of this book, so we, together, can avoid those destructive misunderstandings. Keep in mind that it's hard to recognize that there are other cultures out there compared to your own, but I advise you to **be open** while reading this book that will make the process a lot easier for everyone.[1]

---

1   *When I refer to 'Western Europe' and 'The West,' I am primarily referring to the following countries: Andorra, Austria, Belgium, Denmark, Finland, France, Germany, Greece, Iceland, Ireland, Italy, Liechtenstein, Luxembourg, Malta, Monaco, the Netherlands, Norway, Portugal, San Marino, Spain, Sweden, Switzerland, Turkey, and the United Kingdom.*

Book Structure

As you progress through this book, each chapter will focus on one of the nine skills you need to master in Western professional environments. These chapters aren't just informational – they're designed to be **practical guides,** giving you tools you can immediately apply. You'll find real-life examples, personal stories, exercises, and practical tips to help you internalize each skill.

However, this book isn't meant to be skimmed through. It's important to **pause, reflect, and truly understand** the principles presented. The way we work in the West is different from the way things often operate in India, and understanding these differences requires active engagement.

The book flows logically from one skill to the next, each representing a chapter itself, starting with understanding why adaptation is necessary and moving into more specific skills like **convincing with clear, solution-focused arguments** or **engaging confidently with superiors.** Each chapter is designed to first encourage reflection on cultural differences, followed by step-by-step guidance, ensuring that by the end, you'll have a thorough understanding of how to apply the skill effectively.

However, it's crucial to understand that the nine skills I present here are not meant to replace what you already bring to the table. The abilities and strengths you have developed from your own culture—such as **adaptability, resourcefulness,** and **strong relationship-building**—are incredibly valuable. These skills have helped you succeed in dynamic, often complex environments, and when combined with the lessons in this book, they will make you unstoppable. This book is designed to **complement** your existing strengths, not override them. By integrating these western-oriented skills with the powerful tools you already possess, you'll be able to bridge cultural gaps and thrive on a global stage, standing out as a collaborator in any workplace.

This book is built on my own experience, alongside research from recognized works like *The Culture Map* by **Erin Meyer,** a respected professor at INSEAD and *Speaking of India* by **Craig Storti**, which highlight the broader differences between India and the West. But unlike those books, which focus on helping Westerners understand Indian culture, this book is entirely about helping **you,** as an Indian professional, understand the Western approach. I've also conducted interviews and had in-depth discussions with Indian professionals to pinpoint where cultural gaps are most significant, and from this, I've distilled nine essential skills.

For example, take the story of **Rohan,** a talented colleague who initially struggled with direct communication and engaging with superiors. Through small, intentional changes—like becoming more proactive in meetings and practicing direct communication—Rohan transformed his career. He became more confident, effective, and respected within his Western team. His story proves that mastering these skills is not just possible—it's essential.

The figure below illustrates how each skill builds on the previous ones, creating a strong foundation that leads to effective cross-cultural success.

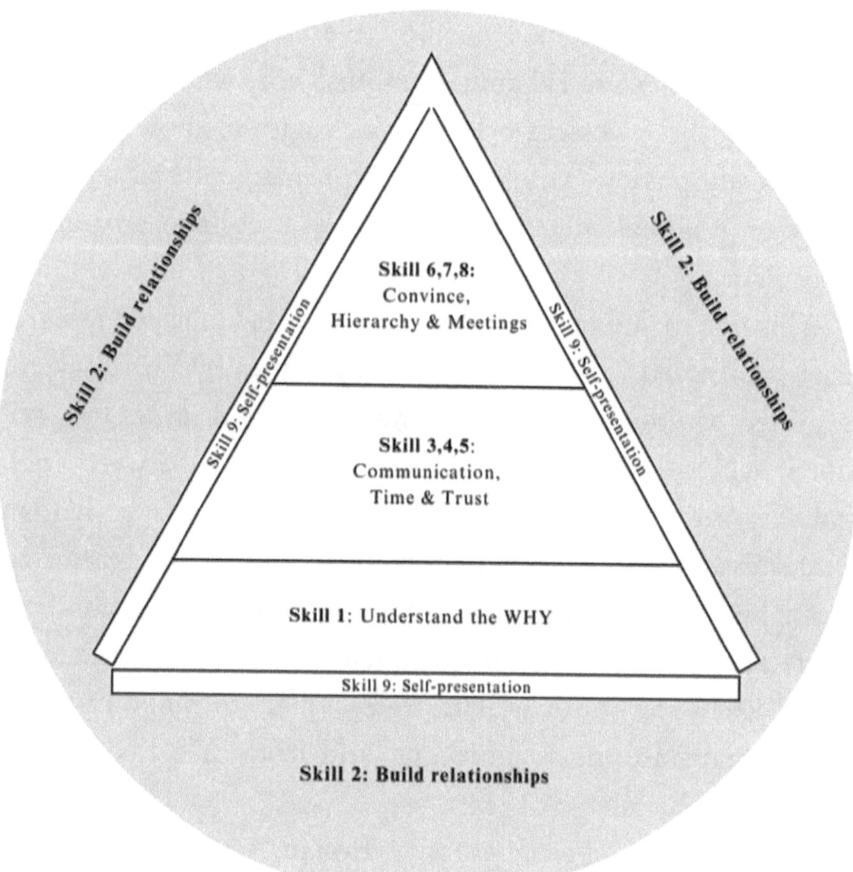

Figure 1.1: *The Nine Skills*

- *Skills 1 and 2 form the foundations. Skill 1 is the essential cornerstone—without it, moving forward is nearly impossible. Skill 2 is the backbone, built and strengthened through every other skill, connecting them all.*
- *Skills 3 through 5 delve into core Western values, offering insights into how they shape work culture, dynamics, and expectations, guiding you on what to adopt and apply.*
- *Skills 6 through 8 builds on the earlier skills, expanding them into critical areas where Western and Indian approaches often differ.*
- *Skill 9 is the glue that holds everything together; without it, even the strongest foundations could crumble.*

Your Journey Starts Here

This book is more than just a collection of advice—it's a **roadmap** to your success in the global workplace. By mastering the nine essential skills outlined here, you're not just learning how to survive in Western business environments; you're equipping yourself to **thrive**. Each of these skills is meant to be learned, practiced, and refined over time—just like any successful habit.

Small, consistent changes can lead to powerful transformations. The skills in this book aren't meant to overwhelm you, but to be implemented step-by-step, just as I've seen professionals like Rohan do. By adopting these skills gradually, you'll start to see how they integrate naturally into your work, making you more confident, effective, and successful with every step.
Your strengths as an Indian professional—adaptability, resilience, analytical thinking, collaborative spirit, and a strong work ethic—are already invaluable. This book isn't about skills you already possess, but rather a new set of skills. By adding these skills to your toolkit, you'll be able to bridge cultural gaps and set yourself apart in any global setting. The world is changing, and those who can bridge cultural divides are the ones who will seize the most valuable opportunities.

So, take this as your first step. **Commit to learning, reflecting, and applying** the skills ahead. With dedication and small, consistent actions, you'll discover that mastering these skills will unlock new opportunities and elevate your career to new heights.

1

The Power of Adaptation: Why Western Norms Matter

ભ✻ભ

Mastering the balance between adapting to Western culture without losing your own identity.

The Invisible Wall

Action Starts With Understanding

You log in for your Monday morning meeting, ready to start with a bit of small talk. After all, this is how you've always built trust—with warmth, familiarity, and a personal touch. As the meeting starts, there's a brief exchange—maybe a quick comment about the weekend or the weather—but it lasts no more than 30 seconds. Before you know it, your western colleagues pivot directly to the agenda, their voices clear and focused. There's no lingering over pleasantries, and time for chit-chat is minimal. You adjust quickly, reminding yourself that in the West, time is money, and efficiency is key. Still, the shift feels jarring, like you're operating by different rules, where every second counts.

As the meeting unfolds, they start discussing a project with a tight deadline. You can already see the cracks forming—the timeline is ambitious, to say the least. You want to speak up, but instead of saying it outright, you choose a more indirect approach. "It seems like we have a lot on our plate," you offer, hoping they'll pick up on the subtle warning. They don't. The conversation moves on, and your concerns get left behind.

In your mind, you've raised the issue. In theirs, nothing's wrong.

The project rolls forward, and you focus on completing the tasks assigned to you. You're diligent, precise, and do exactly what's asked. But while you're waiting for further instructions, your colleagues are moving ahead on their own, anticipating problems, solving them before they arise. They're thinking beyond the immediate task, planning two, three steps ahead. You don't see it at the time, but you're already falling behind—not because you're not working hard, but because you haven't grasped the unspoken expectation that here, you're supposed to take initiative.

Days pass, and the deadline looms closer. You're still confident because you've done everything they asked of you. But then, a crushing realization: you weren't just supposed to complete tasks—you were supposed to anticipate the bigger picture. The urgency hits you like a wave. While you were focused on the tasks at hand, your colleagues had been driving the project forward, thinking ahead, solving problems before they became blockers.

By the time you realize the gravity of the deadline, it's already too late. The project stumbles, and the final results fall short. You wait for some recognition, some acknowledgment of your hard work and dedication—after all, you built relationships, cooperated, and stayed agreeable throughout. But instead, all you receive is disappointment. Your boss expected you to be more than just a passive participant. They were looking for someone who could own the project, voice concerns clearly, and solve problems without needing step-by-step guidance.

You leave the meeting feeling disheartened, and the questions start swirling in your mind. *What went wrong? Why didn't they appreciate my effort?*

But here's the truth: it wasn't just about doing the work. It was about thinking like they do—anticipating problems, managing time with laser focus, and most importantly, speaking up clearly and assertively. In the Western workplace, silence can be misread as inaction and passivity as a lack of leadership. They expect independence, not just compliance. In this environment, it's not enough to do what's asked—you're expected to think ahead, to see what needs to be done next, and take ownership.

You suddenly realize that this isn't just about tasks; it's about mindset. You've been playing by a different set of rules, ones that don't apply in this Western-dominated game. And while it might seem overwhelming, this isn't a failure—it's your wake-up call. This is where your transformation begins.

Imagine what you could achieve if you bridged this cultural gap and mastered the subtle art of blending your strengths with Western professional expectations. No more invisible walls. No more missed opportunities. This is the moment when you can step forward—not just as a participant but as a leader in any room, any country, and any global environment.

This book will show you exactly how to do that.

Why Cultural Differences Exist

Imagine two parallel roads stretching for thousands of years—one in India, the other in the West. Both have faced challenges, achieved greatness, and developed rich cultures. But they've taken different paths, and that's shaped how we live, work, and communicate today.

In India, history is built on relationships. For thousands of years, the focus has been on community and harmony. The influence of religions like Hinduism, Buddhism, and Jainism taught people to seek balance, avoid conflict, and show respect. That's why in your workplaces, you often value keeping the peace over confrontation. It's in the Indian DNA.

Now, compare this to the West. Their story changed dramatically with the Industrial Revolution. In the 18th century, Europe transformed into a productivity machine, driven by efficiency and time management. Suddenly, decisions had to be made fast, results had to be measurable, and progress was everything. This focus on speed and efficiency still shapes how Western companies operate today.

Why does this matter? While Indians inherited a culture that emphasizes patience, indirect communication, and relationships, the Western world values quick decisions, direct feedback, and individual responsibility. Neither is wrong. But in today's global workplace, where these two worlds collide, misunderstandings can cost you your work.

Think about the last time you were in a meeting with Western colleagues. Did you hesitate before voicing a concern? Did you wait to be asked for your opinion rather than offering it freely? That hesitation isn't just a personal trait—it's the product of centuries of cultural evolution. But here's the key: it's something you can overcome.

Recognizing these differences is the first step. But if you want to succeed in today's interconnected world, you need to know how to bridge them. This book will show you exactly how to adapt without losing who you are.

The Consequences of Not Adapting: The Danger of Misunderstandings

Imagine this: you're working on a big project with a Western client. You've put in the hours, built relationships, and made sure everyone's happy. You've done everything you thought was expected of you. But then, the feedback comes in—and it's not what you expected. The client is disappointed, the project is behind schedule, and, worst of all, they're questioning your commitment. Where did it go wrong?

The truth is, they saw things differently from the start. And here's the tricky part: most of the time, **they don't even realize there's a cultural gap.** Just like you, they think their way of doing things is universal. They're not aware that the way you communicate—subtle, indirect, and respectful—could be misinterpreted as uncertainty or a lack of commitment.

Western professionals often aren't aware of these differences. They haven't lived in India, and they don't understand the layers of communication that come naturally to you. To them, directness isn't rude—it's expected. They might not know that when you hesitate before giving a firm 'yes', you're weighing all the factors, trying to avoid overpromising. Instead, they might see that hesitation as indecision.

Misunderstandings like these can quickly spiral out of control, especially in professional relationships. When your client or colleague interprets your actions (or inactions) negatively, it doesn't just affect a single project—it can impact your entire reputation. Contracts fall through. Promotions are passed over.

Respect is lost. All because of a misunderstanding that neither party even realized was happening.

And the risk here isn't just in a single miscommunication. **Repeated misunderstandings can be disastrous.** It's one thing if your Western colleague misinterprets your silence in a meeting once, but if it happens again and again, it starts to affect how they perceive you. You may know you're working hard behind the scenes, but from their perspective, it looks like you're not stepping up, not taking initiative, or not pulling your weight.

Craig Storti, a well-known expert on cross-cultural communication, talks about this in his book on the dangers of misunderstandings. He explains that cultural differences in how we communicate—especially when they go unnoticed—can create lasting damage in professional relationships. These misunderstandings become **barriers** that are difficult to overcome. And once a misunderstanding is ingrained, it's hard to reverse the negative perception that comes with it.

Let's take a real example. You're in a project meeting with Western colleagues. The project is falling behind schedule, and they want to know why. Instead of directly stating the challenges, you hint at the issues, using softer language to avoid placing blame or causing conflict. To you, it's about maintaining harmony and respect for the team. But to them, it looks like you're dodging responsibility. **They're waiting for you to speak up clearly and take ownership.**

When they don't hear that direct, decisive response, they assume you don't fully understand the gravity of the situation— or worse, that you don't care. This gap in understanding leads to frustration. And if it happens often enough, they'll start questioning your competence.

Here's the reality: **Western colleagues and clients may not understand that these differences exist at all.** They're operating under the assumption that everyone communicates and works the same way they do. If you're not adapting to their expectations—speaking up clearly, taking initiative, managing deadlines with urgency—they're likely to interpret this as a lack of competence or engagement.

Before we move forward, it's essential to address some of the common perceptions Westerners have when working with Indians. Understanding these will help us identify where changes can be made and why they matter.

Western colleagues

Western colleagues often say:

- **Indians say 'yes' but don't always mean it.** This creates confusion when tasks don't get done or expectations aren't met.
- **They don't communicate when they're falling behind or missing a deadline.** This leads to unnecessary surprises and rushed fixes.
- **Indians tend to overcommit.** They agree to deadlines they can't realistically meet and take on tasks beyond their capacity.
- **Getting constructive feedback from Indians is difficult.** It's as if they avoid being honest or critical, which makes improvement challenging.
- **They hesitate to act independently.** They frequently ask for permission or approval for things they're more than capable of handling on their own.
- **They rarely admit when they don't understand something.** Even when asked directly, they avoid asking questions, which leads to mistakes later.
- **They don't push back when they disagree.** Whether it's a flawed idea or an unrealistic plan, they stay quiet when we need them to speak up.
- **They might say one thing in a meeting but do something different afterward.**
- **Taking ownership or responsibility seems difficult for them.**

I know you're probably reading this with a raised eyebrow, disagreeing with some or even all of these statements. But here's the truth: these are real concerns that Westerners experience when working with Indians. And this book exists to tackle these very issues and make you understand why they say these things.

On the flip side, you have probably wondered about aspects that Westerners do. Why don't Westerners understand us when we tell them 'no'? Why don't Westerners give us more guidance and instructions? Why are Westerners so abrupt? Why do Westerners always ask for things at the last-minute? Why don't Westerners ever take our suggestions seriously?

The good news? These challenges are not personal failings – they're rooted in cultural misunderstandings. And the better news? By the end of this book, you'll have the tools to clear up those misunderstandings and build stronger, more effective relationships.

Why You Need to Adapt

In an ideal world, both sides would adapt—Western professionals would learn more about Indian culture, and you would learn more about theirs. But in most professional situations, it's often you who needs to take the first step. Why? Because **adapting to your environment is one of the most powerful skills you can develop.** Especially when the business world you're entering into is shaped by Western norms.

It's not about one culture being better than the other, nor is it about losing who you are. It's about recognizing **who sets the expectations** in the business interaction you're in. If the client or decision-maker is based in the West, and naturally, they expect the work to align with the systems they're familiar with.

Imagine you're part of a team of ten people, and you're the only Indian professional. It's unlikely that the entire team will change their communication style or work habits for you—not because they don't value your culture, but because they may not even realize the differences exist. They're operating based on what they know and expect, and it's easier for one to change than ten.

Take the example of working as a consultant for a Western company. They've hired you because of your expertise, but they also expect you to work in a way that aligns with their norms—direct communication, fast decision-making, and clear, measurable outcomes. If you approach the project the way you're used to in India—focusing more on building relationships or using indirect communication to avoid conflict—there's a risk they'll misinterpret that as hesitation or a lack of urgency.

It's not that they don't appreciate your work—it's that they do not fully understand the cues you're giving. And in these situations, **adapting to their expectations ensures your work is understood and valued.**

I experienced this firsthand when I lived and worked in India. I adapted in many ways to align with the local culture. I ate with my hands, worked the 10-6 schedule, and used more indirect language when communicating with colleagues. I saw that in India, relationship-building often came before the work, and I adjusted to that flow. I learned to give feedback more subtly and embraced non-verbal communication styles that were different from what I was used to. In the same way, you'll often find yourself in situations where **you need to adapt.** It's about recognizing the environment you're in and navigating it effectively.

Cultural Understanding Takes Time

It's tempting to think you already understand Western culture. After all, you've been exposed to it your entire life—through movies, TV shows, social media, and maybe even short trips abroad. You've seen how they communicate, how they manage time, and how they handle business.

But here's the reality: **True cultural understanding takes time.** You can't fully grasp the nuances of Western professional behavior by watching films or taking a vacation. These glimpses into Western life only show the surface. The way people behave in a casual, social setting isn't necessarily the way they operate in professional environments.

Think of it this way: Just because someone has watched a Bollywood movie doesn't mean they truly understand the depth of Indian culture—the importance of family, the unspoken rules around respect, or the role of hierarchy in everyday life. The same goes for understanding Western culture. It's much deeper than what you see on the surface. The differences may seem subtle, but they're critical when it comes to succeeding in a professional environment.

For younger Indian generations, the exposure to Western culture is more frequent. You see Western brands, follow Western influencers, and consume Western media. And while this gives you a head start, **it's not enough.** Exposure alone doesn't equal understanding. **You need to actively invest in learning**—whether that's through direct experience working with Western colleagues, studying how decisions are made, or understanding how they approach conflict and deadlines.

Mastering Cultural Skills: Your Edge in a Globalized World

The world has never been more connected. In every industry, from technology to marketing to research, businesses are crossing borders and cultures. And right now, India is at the center of it all.

India's workforce is young, talented, and ready to take on the global stage. The home to some of the world's fastest-growing industries, and Western companies are looking to India to fill critical roles. The West needs Indian talent—but here's the challenge: you're not the only one. Every day, thousands of skilled professionals across India are stepping into this global marketplace. So, how do you stand out?

The answer is simple: master the skills laid out in this book that will give you an edge, trust my words.

Many Indian professionals have worked with the West for years but still struggle to fully understand the nuances of Western business. They excel in their technical skills but miss the mark on communication, decision-making, and leadership styles that Western companies expect. This is where you can set yourself apart.

I've seen this happen repeatedly—Indian professionals who are incredibly skilled but don't reach their full potential because they haven't mastered this one critical skill. But those who do? They succeed like no one else.

India is rising. No longer just participating in the global economy— you're leading it, predicted to soon be the largest economy in the world. But as part of this generation, you have a unique opportunity to take India's progress even further. By mastering these skills, you're not just helping yourself— you're helping elevate India on the world stage.

Why Communication Will Matter Even More in the Age of AI

India has long been known for its ability to handle complex, time-consuming tasks in fields like IT and software development. India is recognized as the **IT outsourcing capital of the world**. The **IT and business process management (BPM) sector** alone generated **$194 billion in revenue** in 2021 .Indian professionals have been the go-to solution for technical expertise and labor-intensive projects for decades.

But the landscape is changing. With the rise of **AI**, many tasks that once required significant time and labor can now be done faster and more efficiently. **AI-assisted coding platforms** and advanced automation tools are enabling companies to handle routine technical work in-house, reducing their reliance on outsourcing for basic tasks.

However, here's the opportunity: Western companies will still prefer to work with Indian professionals—if it's efficient. And now, efficiency goes beyond just technical skills. It's about how well you can communicate, manage expectations, and navigate cultural differences.

India's IT industry remains resilient, with exports from India's technology industry are poised to reach $200 billion, growing at a 3.3% rate year-on-year, showing that India remains the preferred destination for outsourcing and IT services. Western companies value Indian professionals for their ability to deliver high-quality work at scale, but they now demand seamless communication and collaboration to ensure efficiency and success.

The Future is Yours to Shape

India's younger generation is not just part of a global shift—it's leading it. More than **half of India's 1.4 billion people are** under the age of 25, and with a median age of just **29 years,** India is one of the youngest major economies in the world. This positions you—and your peers—at the heart of global growth. The opportunities are endless, but so is the competition.

As India continues to rise on the world stage, your technical skills alone won't set you apart. The real edge lies in **how well you can adapt, communicate, and collaborate** in a world driven by **globalization and AI.** But here's the key: Western companies are looking for more than just technical expertise. **They want smooth, efficient collaboration**—and that's where mastering the skills will make all the difference.

This chapter is the foundation—**Skill 1: Understand that you need to adapt.** The rest of this book will give you the practical tools to thrive in Western environments. Learning to communicate effectively, manage expectations, and navigate cultural differences will not only help you stand out—it will position you to lead.

You're part of a generation that's shaping India's future as a **global leader.** The ability to bridge cultural gaps is a skill that will elevate you above the competition, especially in a world where **AI can automate technical tasks** but cannot replace **human connection and understanding.**

By understanding this first critical lesson—that **adaptation is essential**—you're already on the path to becoming someone who thrives in any environment.

The world is watching. The future is yours. Are you ready?

Skill 1: *Understand the importance of adapting to Western professional norms.*

2

Small Talk, Big Impact: Building Relationships in the West

ও৺ও

Get confident to engage with strangers in light-hearted conversations.

The power of taking initiative - In the West, connections aren't built by waiting—step up, speak out, and let your voice drive new relationships.

Stop the initial stages of formality—boldness breaks barriers, and only those who engage fully will form lasting bonds.

When my friends and family first asked me, "How are your new colleagues from India?" I always found myself talking about how kind, warm, and welcoming they were. Compared to my Scandinavian and Western friends, there was a noticeable openness in their demeanor—friendliness that made them seem instantly approachable. But, despite this warmth, something was missing for me at first: that instant spark of connection. You know the feeling when you meet someone and think, *We could be great friends.* That was something I initially struggled to find in India.

In Norway, we have a saying: "Like barn, leker best"—roughly translated, "Similar children play best together." It's simple: people tend to bond faster with those who share similar values, interests, and energy levels. This makes sense—when you feel like someone understands you, forming friendships becomes almost effortless. So, naturally, it was different connecting with colleagues in India, where interests, and even humor were not always aligned with mine.

But here's the important lesson: those differences didn't mean deeper connections weren't possible. In fact, once I stopped expecting that instant click and started paying attention to the uniqueness of my colleagues, everything changed. I realized that building friendships across cultures isn't about seeking similarity, but about embracing differences. The barriers I first felt weren't insurmountable at all—they just required a shift in perspective. Over time, I developed deep friendships with my Indian colleagues. What began as small talk, cautious and polite, slowly grew into something more—a friendship grounded in understanding and shared experiences, even across cultural lines.

In this chapter, and the second skill, we'll break down those subtle cultural differences that make forming relationships between Westerners and Indians seem tricky at first. But that's just the beginning. Once we understand these differences, I'll share the strategies I used—and ones that I've seen work for others—to bridge those gaps. Whether it's about navigating new communication styles or finding shared ground, these tools will help you create connections that feel authentic and meaningful. And the best part? Once you get past the initial barriers, you'll find that relationships start to flow naturally. The key lies in taking the first step and recognizing that great friendships often come from the unexpected.

Cracking the Code: How Westerners Build Relationships

Story of an Indian in the U.S.

Priya arrived in Seattle brimming with optimism, expecting to build friendships as effortlessly as she had back home in India. In India, connections formed naturally—over meals, conversations, and shared experiences that stretched long into the day. But here, in her new office, something felt different.

Her colleagues were polite and friendly at first, but as the days went by, Priya began to feel an invisible wall between them. They chatted briefly, exchanged smiles, but never went beyond the surface. Lunchtime, which she had imagined as a time to bond, was hurried and impersonal. In just 15 to 30 minutes, her colleagues grabbed their meals, exchanged quick pleasantries, and returned to their desks. There was no lingering over conversation, no real opportunity to connect.

Even in after-work gatherings, the interactions felt distant. She would smile and nod, but the conversations stayed light and never deepened. It felt like there was a social script she wasn't given, a way in that remained out of reach. Her attempts to engage more meaningfully often seemed to fall flat.

Language, too, became a subtle barrier. Though fluent in English, Priya struggled to follow conversations peppered with American idioms and cultural references. Her accent, once a point of pride, now felt like it marked her as an outsider, making it even harder to break through.

What puzzled her most was that her colleagues were never rude or dismissive. They were nice, always friendly—just not inclusive. It was as if the doors to deeper connections were locked, and she didn't have the key.

As weeks turned into months, Priya realized that making friends here wasn't as simple as being polite and showing up. In this new world, building relationships required something more—something she wasn't quite sure how to grasp yet.

Building on Your Natural Strengths in Relationships

As an Indian, you likely have a natural edge in building relationships—possibly even better than most Westerners. Community, family, and friendship are central to daily life in India, and values like warmth, loyalty, and hospitality form the bedrock of any relationship. These qualities resonate globally, so you already know how to nurture deep, lasting connections. This is not different in the west. So, this chapter isn't about long-term relationship-building; you've got that covered.

Instead, we'll focus on the cultural nuances in *starting* relationships. In Western culture, initial interactions are often relaxed and informal—people are comfortable chatting casually with strangers in stores or smiling at people on the street. In India, early conversations with new people are usually marked by respect and formality. Westerners, on the other hand, tend to skip these formalities, engaging freely as if they already know the person.

Take a moment to look at this figure. It illustrates how relationships grow over time in Western and Indian cultures, using two distinct patterns:

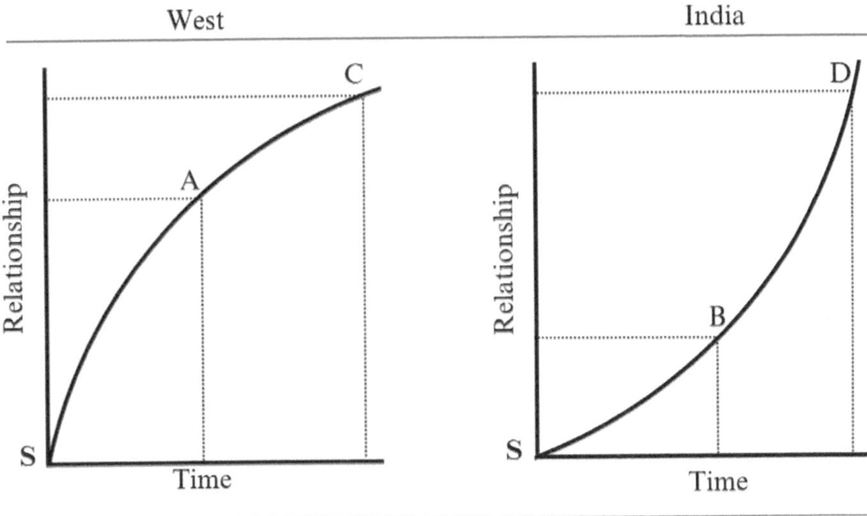

Figure 2.1 Time

The Western model shows how relationships develop quickly. At Point A, rapport has already reached a functional level. This rapid start makes it easy for Westerners to form initial connections—whether for friendships, professional partnerships, or casual social bonds. However, as the curve moves beyond Point A towards Point C, growth begins to slow. The relationship stabilizes, and further depth requires intentional effort.

The Indian model, in contrast, starts more gradually. At Point B, which corresponds to the same timeframe as Point A, rapport is still forming. Conversations and interactions are careful and deliberate, as people take time to assess one another. But once Point B is crossed, the pace of relationship growth accelerates. By the time Point D is reached, the deep connection formed is at the same level as in the West.

Remember that the core values of friendship—mutual trust, loyalty, and warmth—are universal. The difference lies in the journey to reach that level, which depends primarily on the activities, conversations, and shared initiatives between two individuals from the first meeting (Point S) to Points A and B. From Point A to C in the Western model or Point B to D in the Indian model, the process is fundamentally the same, regardless of India or the West.

This chapter will guide you through these early encounters—those first few moments with a new colleague, a potential friend, or a stranger. Once you navigate this initial hurdle, you'll find that you can nurture the relationship with the same warmth and familiarity you bring to your family, friends, and co-workers back home.

This chapter begins with brief stories from my own life that reflect a typical Western way of growing up and forming relationships to enhance your cultural understanding. These insights are important because our upbringing deeply influences how we approach and engage with new people. Through these stories, you'll gain a better understanding of how early encounters with others often unfold in the West and how you can apply these approaches in your own life going forward.

Reflection point: As you read, take a moment to reflect on the similarities and differences between these experiences and your own upbringing. How do the first stages of building relationships usually play out for you?

Cultural Understanding

My childhood: building friendships through shared interests

Growing up in Norway, like many Western countries, friendships are primarily being developed through shared activities outside the home and family circle. From an early age, I learned that building and maintaining friendships was a constant cycle of connection and change.

In kindergarten and elementary school, friendships were forged in the brief 15-30 minute breaks between classes or during quick lunchtime conversations. These moments of bonding were crucial. The kids you connected with most were the ones you invited over after school to hang out, playing soccer or video games until it was time to go home. It was in these small but meaningful exchanges that our friendships deepened, often revolving around shared activities.

As we moved into middle school, our interests began to shift, and so did our friendships. Soccer was no longer the central activity for many of us. Instead, I found myself gravitating toward new hobbies like playing drums in a band or skateboarding with a fresh set of friends. These were the things we did almost every day, and they became the foundation of new connections. What I loved most was the freedom we had to explore our interests independently of our families—this sense of independence was key in forming friendships that lasted.

By the time high school rolled around, our social lives expanded even more. At 16, I began to feel like an adult, and the weekends took on a new meaning. It wasn't just about soccer or band practice anymore. We'd gather for parties where we experimented with alcohol—a common occurrence in many Western cultures, where testing boundaries happens well before the legal drinking age of eighteen. This freedom to socialize without adult supervision was another step in deepening those friendships. I even met my first serious girlfriend at one of these parties, and before long, we were living together—something quite common in the West, even before marriage.

Reflection point: Think about your upbringing and compare it to mine. Reflect on the way you made friends growing up—what drove those connections?

The lesson here is simple: in Western cultures, friendships are built through shared interests and experiences that extend far beyond family. Sports, hobbies, and social gatherings create the strongest and most lasting connections. Unlike in India, where family plays a central role in shaping friendships, western relationships are often independent of family influence. This pattern of friendship-building starts in childhood and extends well into adulthood.

Even now, as an adult, I notice that most of my relationships are shaped by common interests. Whether it's professional networking or personal relationships, the conversation almost always begins with small talk about a shared hobby. In fact, I've found that within just 5 to 15 minutes of conversation, you can often establish a connection with someone based on mutual interests. Whether at work or in social settings, finding this common ground is the key to forming bonds that can last a lifetime.

How I met my friend Daniel

I had just started at a new university and didn't know many people—only three, to be exact. I knew that the best way to form new friendships was to put myself out there, so I did just that. I would introduce myself to people sitting next to me in class or in the canteen. One day, I noticed Daniel chatting with a mutual friend, Simen. Without waiting for Simen to introduce me, I walked over and introduced myself directly: "Hello, my name is Lars. Nice to meet you." We started with small talk, naturally leading to a discussion about our hobbies. We both had a keen interest in working out at the gym, and even though we had just met, Daniel invited me to join him for a workout that afternoon. I was thrilled, as I didn't have many friends yet, and that was the beginning of a great friendship. For the next three years, we worked out together almost every day, and we remain close friends ten years later.

This experience with Daniel highlights a key lesson: relationships, even deep and lasting ones, can be formed in a matter of minutes. By simply taking the initiative, being open, and finding common ground, what begins as small talk can quickly evolve into a meaningful connection. My willingness to reach out and engage can lead to strong bonds that last for years.

Reflection point: Reflect for a moment on how you met your best friend.

My First Job

After completing my first three years of study, I was ready to apply for a prestigious role in Norway. Many large corporations in Norway offer what's called a 'summer internship', and for the particular job I applied to, there were 300 applicants for just one position. I made it through the first round of interviews, then the second, and finally, I reached the last interview with one of the partners, Tom.

I expected the interview to focus on my background and experience. It was scheduled to last 30 minutes, and I had prepared my answers and questions in advance.

We entered a small meeting room where the interview would take place. As we sat down, Tom surprised me by saying there were no set questions or a fixed time for the conversation – he hadn't prepared any specific questions. I had proven my technical expertise in the two former rounds, and now were simply there to get to know each other. This unexpected approach caught me off guard but also made me feel more at ease, as I enjoy leading conversations and engaging in small talk.

I began with the usual topics: a bit about myself, my past experiences and the challenges I'd faced. While I was talking, I kept an eye on Tom, trying to gauge his interest. He shared about his background and field of expertise, which, coincidentally, was one of my favorite subjects. However, I sensed that he was still a bit bored. I realized I needed to make the conversation more engaging for him.

We all enjoy talking about things that interest us, so I decided to ask him about work-life balance—a topic that's important in Western culture, where having interests outside of work is highly valued. When he mentioned skateboarding, I knew we had found common ground. Though it seemed random, I saw an opportunity. I had been into skateboarding when I was 15, and even though I hadn't touched a skateboard in years, I seized the chance to bond over it.

I started asking him more about skateboarding, and I saw a spark of happiness in his eyes. For those 10 minutes, I was a passionate skateboard enthusiast again. Through this shared interest, we discovered other common hobbies, like skiing and hiking. Before we knew it, 60 minutes had passed. As you might have guessed, I got the job. While my qualifications and grades played a role, it was my ability to connect with Tom over shared interests that ultimately helped me secure the position.

This method of bonding over shared interests, as described in the story, is something I use frequently. Whether in my personal life to make friends, at work with colleagues, or even when I met my first girlfriend, identifying and connecting through hobbies has always been key. If you want to build a relationship with someone from the West, try to find their hobbies and see if there's a connection with something you enjoy.

The Unseen Barriers

The next section focuses on the unseen barriers you need to understand in order to bridge the gap effectively.

Independence and Family Dynamics

In Western countries, independence and being your own person are among the most vital aspects of life. Achieving self-reliance is seen as a significant milestone. From an early age, parents encourage their children to become self-reliant, knowing that by the time they turn 18, they will likely move out and start living on their own. This means earning their own money, taking care of themselves, and managing all aspects of life independently.

For example, I moved out of my parents' home when I was eighteen to join the military for a year. After that, I moved to Kristiansand to pursue a bachelor's degree in economics, and later returned to my hometown at age 23 to complete my master's in finance. Even when I moved back to the same city as my parents, living with them was never an option. This reflects a common practice in the West, where young adults are expected to live independently, even if they are geographically close to their families.

This stands in contrast to how it often is in India, where joint families are still common, and living with one's parents is perfectly normal. Naturally, this affects how people spend their free time and experience with forming new relationships. For someone like me, who lives alone, I have no obligations other than to myself, and my decisions are typically made with my needs in mind.

In Indian culture, family often plays a role in shaping and supporting friendships. This approach reflects a deeply interconnected way of life, where social bonds often extend beyond individuals to include families and communities. In contrast, Westerners grow up learning to build friendships independently. With little involvement from family, they've spent their whole lives putting themselves out there, taking initiative, and forming connections on their own.

Inclusion and exclusion

In my conversations with people from India and the West, a common observation often arises: making friends in Western cultures can be challenging, even for the locals, especially for newcomers. Dhara's experience perfectly illustrates this point.

When Dhara moved from India to the U.S., she was filled with excitement and anticipation. Back home, community was everything—neighbors and co-workers were like family, and friendships formed naturally in these environments. However, while everyone was polite and friendly in the U.S, Dhara soon noticed a pattern: these interactions rarely went beyond surface-level pleasantries. Invitations to join activities or social gatherings were few and far between unless she made the first move. Over time, Dhara found herself gravitating toward the Indian community, where she found the warmth and connection she was used to. But she couldn't help feeling a sense of disappointment that her efforts to form friendships with locals didn't seem to lead anywhere.

This experience isn't unique to Dhara—it reflects a broader trend in many Western societies. Here, newcomers often find it challenging to break into existing social circles. The responsibility to fit in and make connections largely falls on the *'new guy'* rather than on the established group.

This is very different from my experiences in Mumbai. There, people were incredibly welcoming, making it easy to feel part of the community right away. My Indian friend Rohan and I discussed this, and we both noticed how much more open people in India are to including newcomers. In India, There's a saying, *"Tradition and a norm that any guest who comes to your home is like a god in another form,"* so they're treated with immense respect and honor, making them feel extra special. There is no such saying in the west, unfortunately.

Take the first step—build connections with your colleagues instead of waiting for them to come to you.

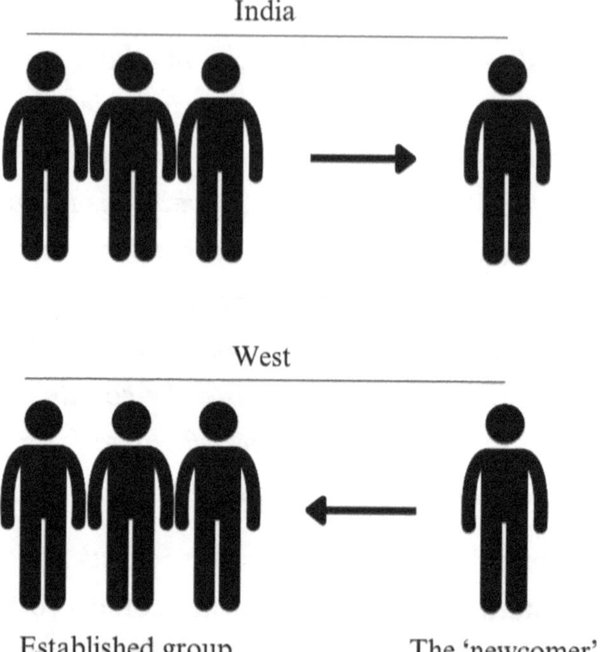

Figure 2.2 Inclusiveness

In Western countries, people often greet newcomers with a friendly introduction, but in many cases, the connection doesn't progress beyond that. After the initial welcome, it's usually up to the newcomer to take the initiative to join in and get to know others more deeply. This can be challenging, and I've seen new employees at our company or new students at school struggle to build lasting friendships. For someone from India, where the community tends to fully embrace newcomers, this difference can lead to misunderstandings. They might arrive expecting the same level of ongoing warmth and inclusion they're used to back home, but in the West, the responsibility to deepen those connections typically falls on them. The initial welcome is genuine, but forming meaningful relationships requires the newcomer to actively reach out and engage further. If you are starting a job in the West, there tends to be a reliance on your self-sufficiency, with an emphasis on the individual's responsibility to adapt.

Understanding these cultural differences is crucial. It helps everyone be more understanding and makes it easier for people moving between these cultures to adjust and build friendships.

Dhara's turning point came during a coffee break conversation with Emily, an American colleague who had become one of her few acquaintances. Dhara shared her experiences and her longing to build more diverse friendships. Emily listened intently, nodding in recognition. "It's not just you," Emily said. "I think sometimes we Americans wait for new folks to take the initiative. It's not that we're not interested in getting to know you; it's just that we often don't think to extend the invitation."

This conversation was a revelation to Dhara. It wasn't that she wasn't wanted; it was a cultural mismatch in how friendships are formed. Armed with this new understanding, Dhara began to approach her social interactions differently. She took the lead in inviting colleagues and neighbors to join her for outings. To her delight, many accepted, and friendships slowly began to bloom.

Through her journey, Dhara learned that building bridges across cultures sometimes requires being the architect of your own social circle. It was a valuable lesson in the power of taking initiative and a reminder of the beauty in the diverse ways friendships are formed around the world. She realized that while the approach to friendship might vary from one country to another, the underlying desire for connection and understanding is a universal human trait.

Formal vs. Informal

In a conversation with my Indian colleague, Arjun Patel, I realized just how different forming friendships can be in the West compared to India. In Western cultures, making new friends—even in professional settings—is often an informal process from the start. While the approach outside of work might be a bit different, the core idea remains the same.

The Story of Arjun: Embracing Informality

When Arjun Patel moved from New Delhi to San Francisco, he was excited yet anxious to start his new job at a leading tech firm. Back in India, Arjun was accustomed to a more formal way of building relationships, where respect for titles and a certain decorum were key. This had always served him well in making connections, both professionally and personally.

On his first day, Arjun dressed in a sharp suit, a stark contrast to his colleagues' casual jeans and t-shirts. He greeted everyone with a polite "Good morning," waiting for formal introductions before engaging further. To him, this was the respectful way to enter a new environment.

But as the days turned into weeks, Arjun noticed something unsettling. While his colleagues were polite, their interactions with him didn't move beyond basic courtesies. During lunch, he watched as groups naturally formed, sharing laughter and personal stories. Despite his efforts to maintain professionalism, Arjun found himself on the sidelines, unsure how to break into these circles.

The turning point came when Jake, his manager, invited Arjun out for a Friday night gathering. Hesitant but curious, Arjun accepted, unsure of what to expect. The casual atmosphere of the local bar was a stark contrast to what he was accustomed to. There were no assigned seats or formal introductions—just open conversations and shared stories, with everyone there, from the company's founder to the interns, laughing together. It reminded Arjun of family gatherings back home, where he and his cousins would laugh and chat freely, bridging gaps effortlessly.

At first, Arjun felt out of place, sticking to his reserved demeanor. But as the evening wore on, he realized that the informality wasn't a lack of respect; it was a way to break down barriers. Encouraged by the relaxed environment, Arjun decided to share a funny story from back home. To his surprise, it was met with genuine laughter and interest. In that moment, he understood that in this culture, openness and informality were the keys to forming connections.

Embracing this new approach, Arjun began to engage more freely with his colleagues. He asked about their weekends, joined in on lunch outings, and even suggested a cricket match—a nod to his roots. His efforts didn't go unnoticed. Before long, he found himself part of a close-knit group that appreciated him for who he was.

The narrative of Arjun Patel illustrates the cultural divide between the formal, hierarchical norms of Indian society and the informal, egalitarian approach favored in the West.

At the core of Arjun's initial struggle is the deeply ingrained Indian cultural norm that values formality, respect, and a procedural approach to both personal and professional relationships. In India, social interactions are often guided by a nuanced understanding of hierarchy, respect for elders and superiors, and the use of formal titles. This formality extends into the professional realm, where formal introductions, attire, and communication styles are not just preferred but expected.

In contrast, the Western approach emphasizes informality. Relationships, whether personal or professional, often develop through spontaneous interactions, shared experiences, and a mutual exchange of stories. The focus is on individualism and authenticity, rather than one's position within a social or professional hierarchy. This cultural ethos values ease of communication and approachability, viewing them as the foundation for trust and rapport.

You should note that the formal and respectful approach across hierarchy that is customary in India can be easily misinterpreted in the West. Westerners, unaccustomed to being addressed with titles like 'Mr.' or being approached with excessive formality, may feel uncomfortable. This discomfort can quickly create barriers that hinder the development of friendships or close working relationships.

Reflecting on my own experience, I recall when I first moved to India. Every time I met someone new, I was introduced through a third-party, even if it was just a colleague sitting under the same roof. This was quite different from what I was used to back home, where third-party introductions are reserved for very formal events or business settings. At social gatherings or parties, it's common for individuals to introduce themselves rather than rely on someone else to make the introduction.

Don't wait to be introduced — step forward and introduce yourself, even to strangers.

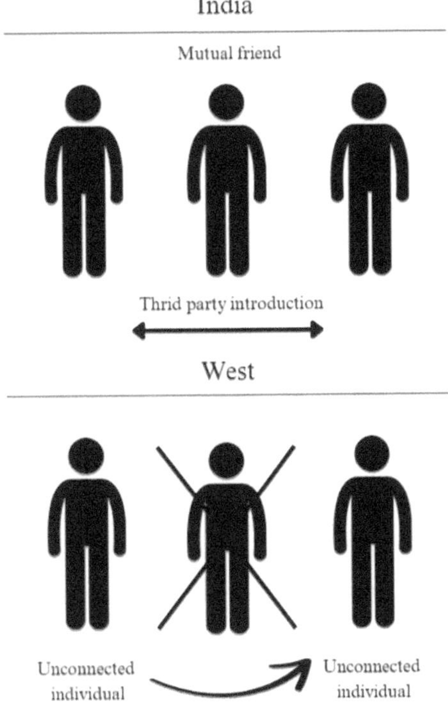

Figure 2.3 Third party introductions

Peach and Coconut

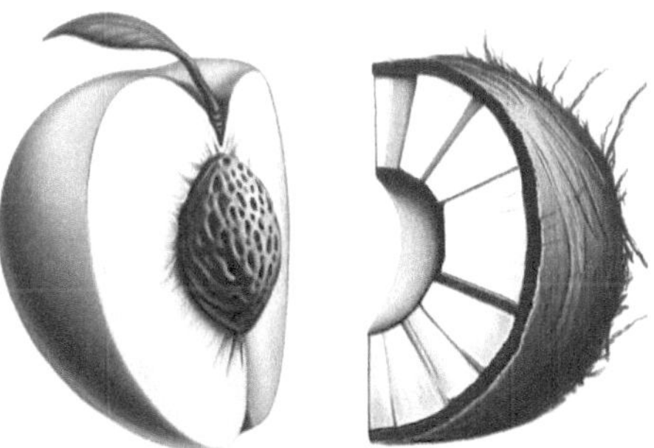

To summarize the pointers from this chapter, Kurt Lewin, a pioneering social psychologist, introduced a powerful metaphor to explain different cultural approaches to relationships and social interaction: the peach and the coconut.

Lewin's study says that in many Western cultures, people are often compared to peaches. This means that they tend to have a 'soft exterior', making them appear approachable, friendly, and open during casual interactions. It's not uncommon for strangers to strike up conversations, and politeness flows easily in social settings. However, beneath that welcoming outer layer lies a 'hard core'. Getting past casual pleasantries and into the realm of deeper, more meaningful relationships often takes time. While Westerners may be quick to engage in friendly chatter, forming true personal connections is a slower process, requiring a strong foundation of trust built through time and shared experiences.

Moreover, Lewin's study found that in many Asian cultures, including India, China, and Japan, people are often described as coconuts. These cultures may seem to have a tougher exterior; initial interactions can feel formal or distant. It may take time, patience, and genuine effort to 'break through' this shell. But once you do, you're welcomed into a much deeper, warmer, and more personal connection. Relationships in coconut cultures are built slowly, but once established, they are strong, enduring, and emotionally rich. These bonds are resilient and often last a lifetime.

Bridging the Gap

Now that we've explored the cultural differences that can make forming relationships a bit tricky for Indians in a Western context, let's shift our focus to what really matters: how to overcome these challenges. The answer is clear; start by visualize a timeline, where each culture has its own starting point.

When it comes to building friendships, Indians often begin with two important steps: formality and respect. Relationships start with careful introductions, polite exchanges, and a gradual buildup of trust. In the West, however, these first steps are usually skipped. Westerners tend to dive straight into casual, open interactions—quickly breaking the ice and creating a friendly atmosphere.

To form friendships more easily with Westerners, try easing up on the formality at the beginning. Approach conversations with a friendly, casual tone, and don't hesitate to share a bit about yourself early on. Westerners appreciate this openness; it builds comfort and makes the relationship feel natural right from the start. While these initial steps might feel different, they're simply a shortcut to reaching the same close, genuine connections you're used to.

The figure below illustrates how Indians tend to take two extra steps when forming new relationships compared to Westerners. The simplest approach? Try skipping these initial formalities and move directly to the comfort stage. While this shift might feel a bit unfamiliar, imagine yourself in the shoes of a Westerner and embrace their fast-paced approach to relationship-building. This is what they're used to and will help you connect more naturally from the start.

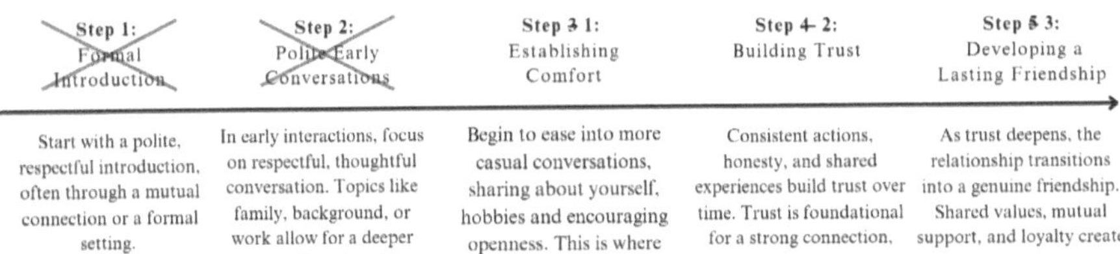

Figure 2.4 Friendship timeline West vs. India

You might wonder, but how do I start right at step 3? If you're used to a gradual, slower development before getting comfortable with someone, this can feel like a big leap. The key is to quickly identify a common interest, as we discussed earlier in the chapter. Finding this shared ground will help steer the relationship in a direction that feels natural. So how do you uncover that common interest subtly and effectively? You do it by mastering the art of small talk, which is what the rest of this chapter will focus on.

Skip the steps of formalities - Treat every first meeting like you're reconnecting with an old friend.

Nurturing common interests

One effective way to start building trust is by finding and nurturing common interests. Patel, a seasoned professional from India, used this simple yet powerful approach with great success during his time in New Zealand. He shared an insightful story about how this strategy worked for him and how it could work for others.

When Patel retired and left New Zealand, he was replaced by Rohan, a younger Indian colleague with an impressive track record in India but limited experience working outside of his home country. Rohan was working tirelessly to secure a promising deal with a potential client in New Zealand. Despite his dedication—crafting a flawless presentation and offering generous terms—the client remained hesitant. After several months of little progress, Rohan reached out to Patel for advice.

In response, Patel flew to Wellington to meet the client face-to-face. As they sat down for their meeting, Patel immediately noticed a rugby ball prominently displayed on the client's desk. Remembering his own days playing rugby in school, Patel seized the opportunity to connect on a personal level by sharing stories from the field. The conversation flowed naturally, moving from thrilling victories to heartbreaking losses, united by the universal language of sports.

However, Patel was mindful of the client's time and knew how valuable it was. After a few moments of personal connection, he skillfully steered the conversation back to business, respecting the client's schedule and focusing on the key points of their proposal. This approach demonstrated Patel's awareness of the client's priorities, balancing personal rapport with professional efficiency.

As their meeting drew to a close, the client mentioned a local rugby match happening that evening and invited Patel to join him. He recognized this as a golden opportunity to deepen their bond and eagerly accepted the invitation. The match was exhilarating, and they spent the evening immersed in the lively atmosphere. Later, over dinner, Patel had more time to further discuss the proposal in a relaxed setting.

The next morning, they met again. The client began by saying, "After our chat and enjoying the match together, I've had a chance to reflect on your proposal. I see the value in what you're offering, and I'm ready to move forward. I just need to run it by my team, but I'm confident we can finalize the details today." True to his word, by the time Patel was boarding his flight back to India, a confirmation email awaited him, signifying the successful closure of the deal.

This story isn't just about Patel's adaptability or finding shared interests; it's a testament to the power of personal connection.

Patel understood something vital: finding common ground—whether it's through rugby or any shared interest—can transform professional relationships into partnerships built on trust and mutual respect. But don't let this example fool you; forming the relationship was important, but equally important were his skills of persuasion, time management, and earning trust to showcase past success, skills we will discuss more later in this book.

Small Talk

The first step in building relationships with someone from the West is mastering the art of small talk. Small talk is the skill of engaging in light, informal conversation, much like the soft hum of background music that makes any social setting more comfortable. It's a critical tool because it acts as a bridge to deeper relationships and meaningful exchanges. When you're good at small talk, you're not just filling silence; you're laying the groundwork for trust and understanding. This can lead to stronger professional networks, richer friendships, and a deeper understanding of the people around you.

There are numerous books dedicated to mastering this vital skill, but this isn't one of them. However, there are quick and easy steps to consider if you want to improve your small talk game. In the West, small talk often revolves around the weather—whether you're in an elevator, meeting someone on the bus, or chatting in line, the go-to topic is usually the weather. But that's not the kind of small talk that will help you build meaningful relationships. Great small talk happens when you hit the right topic, something that both parties are genuinely interested in, and you find that connection quickly.

I experienced this type of small talk just yesterday. It was Thursday, and I was heading to a weekly meeting with one of the directors, Nikolai, a Frenchman who had moved to Norway. Before the meeting, he suggested we grab a coffee. I don't know Nikolai on a personal level, but I realized we were about to spend 10 minutes making small talk, which can be tricky when you're not familiar with someone. As we stood outside the elevator, I knew I needed to find a topic to discuss. Not knowing much about him, I decided to start with something I care about—not because I love talking about it (though I do), but because if he also shares the interest, we'd find common ground.

I mentioned the upcoming tryout for our division's running group, knowing the 'runners' in the office were excited about it. Nikolai is 55 years old, so I hadn't heard him talk about running before, and it seemed like a bit of a stretch. At first, he said he hadn't heard about it, and his body language suggested he wasn't particularly interested. I thought I had missed the mark and was ready to move on to another topic. But before I did, I made a final joke: "So, are you sure you don't want to join the tryout next week?" This was an attempt to lighten the mood and maybe get a laugh—and it worked. To my surprise, Nikolai responded, "If it was 20 years ago, I would, and I'd probably win."

It turns out Nikolai is a former runner with four marathons under his belt. The next 10 minutes were filled with his stories from back in the day, from his training routines to tales of old girlfriends he met through running. I was genuinely interested in hearing his stories and kept the conversation going by asking open-ended questions like, "Tell me about how you trained" and "Why did you quit running?" I shared some of my own experiences but focused on being a good listener—asking follow-up questions and showing that I was paying attention to what he was saying.

The moral of the story is that in just 10 minutes of small talk, I learned more personal stories about Nikolai than I ever knew before. We've now started a new chapter in our friendship that we can build on going forward, and the barriers to communicating with him—both professionally and personally—have been lowered. All of this was achieved through a shared interest and small talk.

10 Steps to Mastering Small Talk

Purpose: This guide is designed to help you navigate the early stages of conversation, focusing on how to make a strong first impression and build rapport through effective small talk.

1. **Initiate with Common Ground:** Start conversations with universally relatable topics like the weather, the event you're attending, or something noticeable in your surroundings. These topics help ease into the conversation without feeling forced.

2. **Ask Open-Ended Questions:** Use questions that encourage more than just a yes-or-no answer. This could involve asking about opinions, experiences, or feelings on a topic. Open-ended questions invite dialogue and demonstrate genuine interest in the other person's thoughts.

3. **Listen Actively:** Pay close attention to what the other person is saying. Show that you're listening through nods, maintaining eye contact, and offering relevant follow-up questions or comments. Active listening is crucial as it makes the other person feel valued and understood.

4. **Share About Yourself:** While it's important to listen, sharing your own experiences and thoughts in moderation creates a balanced conversation. This helps the other person learn about you, paving the way for deeper connections.

5. **Keep It Light and Positive:** Especially in initial interactions, keep the conversation light and positive. Avoid controversial topics and focus on subjects that are enjoyable for both parties, setting a pleasant tone for the conversation.

6. **Practice Empathy and Sensitivity:** Be mindful of cultural differences and sensitivities. Understanding and respecting diverse perspectives can enhance conversations and prevent misunderstandings, which is key in a multicultural environment.

7. **Use Humor Wisely:** A bit of humor can make conversations more enjoyable, but it's important to use it appropriately. Ensure that your humor is inclusive and not at the expense of others, keeping the atmosphere friendly and comfortable.

8. **Be Aware of Non-Verbal Cues:** Pay attention to body language, both yours and the other person's. Non-verbal cues can indicate if the person is engaged or if they feel uncomfortable, allowing you to adjust the conversation as needed.

9. **Mind the Exit:** Know how to gracefully exit a conversation. This might involve summarizing what you've discussed, mentioning a follow-up, or simply expressing appreciation for the chat. A smooth exit leaves a positive lasting impression.

10. **Practice Regularly:** Like any skill, small talk improves with practice. Engage in conversations regularly, reflect on what works well, and continuously refine your approach. The more you practice, the more natural and effective your small talk will become.

Of course, one of the most important aspects of small talk is having topics to discuss. For someone from India, the subjects might differ slightly from those commonly discussed in the U.S., Norway, Australia, or the U.K., but there are universal areas that work well everywhere—such as news, hobbies, work, and technology. The key challenge is finding what you and the other person have in common. If you manage to identify a shared interest quickly, you've made a valuable connection.

Take the story of Nikolai and me, for instance. There was certainly an element of luck that he happened to be passionate about running, which made our conversation flow easily. However, sometimes you may encounter someone with whom you don't share any obvious common ground, and that's perfectly okay. Not every interaction will lead to a deep connection or a lasting relationship. But even in those situations, maintaining a friendly and positive tone can still help foster a respectful and cordial relationship.

Even when you're preparing for a meeting with someone, it's important to do some research on the people you'll be meeting. A great example of this is former U.S. President Barack Obama. During an interview, Jens Stoltenberg, the former Prime Minister of Norway and current NATO leader, reflected on his last meeting with Obama. He said, "We were discussing Afghanistan, Ukraine, military expenses, but what I remember most was how interested he was in my passion for skiing. We spent a lot of time talking about it between meetings." "I was truly impressed by how well he had read up on all the people who came to visit him."

This illustrates how Barack Obama, known for his strong interpersonal skills, frequently uses this technique to connect with others. By finding a shared interest and engaging in that topic, he builds rapport, creating a bond that deepens the relationship.

Below are universal conversation topics that resonate well across both Western and Indian cultures. Choose the ones you feel genuinely interested in, as this will make your small talk feel authentic and natural:

Education and Aspirations
Education is a respected value in both the West and India, making it an easy conversation starter. Ask your colleagues

about their educational background or share your own career aspirations.

Technology and Innovation

Tech is a global language. Conversations around innovation, startups, or even recent technological advancements can spark interest. Discuss trends like artificial intelligence or the future of tech and ask for their thoughts.

Travel and Exploration

The love for travel bridges many cultures. Share stories of places you've been or want to visit. Ask for recommendations or exchange cultural insights.

Entertainment and Media

Movies, music, and sports are universally loved. Whether it's Hollywood or Bollywood, this can be a rich ground for discussion. Feel free to bring up popular films or series—such as The Shawshank Redemption or Inception—to provide insight into Western culture while also bonding over shared entertainment.

Food

Talking about food is one of the simplest ways to connect. Whether it's discussing favorite dishes or different culinary traditions, the conversation can easily flow around common dining habits. Share what you love to eat or ask about their favorite dishes.

Current Events

Discussing recent news or global events offers a broader perspective. Hot topics like climate change, global trends, or recent tech conferences provide material for engaging, thought-provoking conversations.

Sports Events

From cricket to football, sports are a universal way to bond. Share your interest in popular sports from your culture or ask about theirs. International events like the FIFA World Cup or Olympics often spark passionate conversations.

Professional Experience

Workplace challenges, leadership lessons, or industry insights are valuable topics to explore. Ask questions like, "What's your favorite part of your job?" or "How did you get into this field?" These topics often help you understand someone's professional journey and foster a sense of camaraderie.

Taking the initiative in a conversation can feel daunting, but it's one of the most effective ways to break the ice and build rapport—especially when working remotely with colleagues from another culture. Here's an example of how to effortlessly lead a conversation and then smoothly transition into the main topic.

Arjun's Story:

Arjun had always been cautious in conversations with his Western colleagues, often waiting for the right moment to speak. But today, he decided to take the plunge and initiate. He dialed into a meeting with Hans, a project manager from Germany.

"Hey Hans!" Arjun greeted him with a smile. "How's everything going in Germany? Still getting that perfect running weather?"

Hans laughed, instantly warming up to the conversation. "Yeah, sunny and 15 degrees today. Perfect for a run later! How's the weather where you are?"

Arjun felt the conversation flowing easily now. "It's warm here too, but we're more used to the sun than you guys! You must be looking forward to a run after work."

This wasn't just idle talk—it was Arjun connecting. In the past, he might have jumped straight to the meeting agenda, but today he decided to explore more. "Out of curiosity, Hans, what do you enjoy most on days like this—running or maybe firing up the grill with some friends?"

"Oh, a bit of both," Hans replied, clearly pleased. "Running, then maybe a barbecue with a few close friends. How about you? Any big plans?"

This was Arjun's chance to create a stronger bond. "I'm actually trying to improve my stamina for cricket. Do you have any tips for building endurance?"

Arjun didn't realize it, but in just a few short minutes, he'd done more than engage in small talk – he'd found common ground. He was already learning something valuable from Hans, a tip for his training routine. But most importantly, Arjun had unlocked the power of building rapport: he had shown interest in Hans's life and shared something personal in return. This kind of connection makes working together smoother, as you feel more like a team.

As the conversation shifted toward the project, Arjun could sense a difference. The tone was warmer, more relaxed, and there was trust in the air—a trust built through genuine connection, not just shared tasks. "By the way, regarding our project," Arjun transitioned smoothly, "I'd love to hear about your preferred work style. Any particular approaches you find effective?"

Hans responded eagerly, and the meeting took off.

Next time you're working with a Western colleague, try starting the conversation with a simple, engaging question. Build off their response and share a little about yourself. In no time, you'll notice that these interactions help the rest of your workflow much more naturally.

Stand Tall, Speak Loud, Your Voice, Your Power

Developing meaningful relationships, especially across cultures, is not just about following a set of formalities—it's about taking initiative, being bold, and breaking free from Indian traditions that may hold you back. In this chapter, we've talked about engaging in small talk and confidently stepping into new situations.

In the West, friendships and professional connections aren't built on how respectful or formal you can be – they're founded on openness, confidence, and the courage to connect. Being reserved or overly deferential can make it hard for others to see you as an equal, and in a business environment, it may prevent you from gaining the respect you deserve. If you place yourself too low in the hierarchy, you'll struggle to create real friendships and authentic connections. So, skip those initial stages of formality and jump right to the stage where you already feel you know the person.

Here's a roadmap for moving forward with confidence, toning down formality, and actively engaging with new people:

Step 1: Initiative Over Formality

Break free from the instinct to wait for others to initiate. In the West, confidence and proactive behavior are admired, so take the lead—whether in conversation or collaboration. Don't wait for an invitation; create the moment and shed excessive politeness. Showing initiative and bringing your true self forward will set you apart.

Step 2: Bold Conversations

Forget hierarchy in your interactions. Whether speaking to a CEO or a peer, approach them with curiosity and openness. The key to strong connections is being genuine, so engage in small talk, share your experiences, and don't shy away from asking questions. People will respect you more for your authenticity and willingness to connect.

Step 3: Embrace Openness

Be curious about their culture, and confidently share your own. Don't hesitate to discuss your background, thinking it may be less relevant or valuable. Westerners appreciate authenticity, and sharing your story will only strengthen the bond. Own your culture and bring it to the conversation as a point of pride.

Step 4: Confidence in Your Value

Recognize that you bring immense value to the table—both professionally and personally. Stop putting others on a pedestal; your experiences, ideas, and personality are equally valuable. Embracing your worth changes the dynamic, allowing others to see you with more respect. Confidence in your value will shift how others perceive you and how you engage.

Priya's Journey: Stepping Up

When Priya arrived in Seattle, the city's skyline felt both vast and isolating. Every morning, as she walked into her tech office, she was greeted by the hum of conversations that didn't include her. She was used to the busyness, the subtle nods exchanged in the office kitchen, but there was a heaviness in the silence between her and her colleagues.

Priya wasn't shy, but she was careful. Too careful, perhaps. In meetings, she'd wait for her turn to speak, measuring her words, never wanting to seem too forward. Politeness was deeply ingrained in her, and she didn't want to break the unwritten rules of this new culture she found herself in. Yet, after months of the same routine, she realized that no deeper connections were forming. She began to question herself. Was she not interesting enough? Not fun enough? Or was it just that her colleagues already had their circles and weren't open to letting her in?

The Moment of Clarity

It wasn't until one afternoon, after a year of quiet lunches and surface-level conversations, that Priya experienced her turning point. She was sitting at her desk when she overheard two colleagues planning a weekend hike. "That sounds like fun," she thought to herself. Her immediate instinct was to stay quiet—what if she was intruding? What if they didn't really want her to come? But then she realized something that hit her deeply: the only reason she wasn't part of their plans was because she hadn't made an effort to be.

In that moment, Priya made a decision. She wasn't going to wait to be invited into people's lives anymore. She wasn't going to stay on the sidelines, waiting for someone to notice her or break the ice. Taking a deep breath, she walked over to her colleagues and said with a smile, "That hike sounds incredible. Mind if I join?" It felt bold, almost too bold for her, but the reaction surprised her. Her colleagues looked up, smiling, and said, "Of course! We'd love for you to come."

That small moment of stepping outside her comfort zone was all it took to change the trajectory of her experience. It wasn't just about a hike; it was about realizing that she had the power to create her own opportunities for connection.

Finding Boldness in Conversations

The next day, Priya found herself at a team lunch, sitting across from one of her newer colleagues, Emily. Normally, Priya would wait for someone else to start the conversation, but this time, she took the lead. "You know, back in India, we have these massive family gatherings, especially during Diwali," she said. "Everyone comes together—it's loud, chaotic, but beautiful. What's your family's favorite tradition?"
Emily's face lit up, and soon they were swapping stories about their families, laughing about childhood memories. The bond that had seemed impossible to create only a few weeks ago now began to form naturally. Priya realized that her colleagues weren't closed off – they were simply waiting for someone to take the first step.

The Power of Cultural Exchange

Encouraged by her small victories, Priya decided to fully embrace the beauty of her Indian heritage. She invited her team to celebrate Diwali at her home—a bold move, considering how different this tradition was from anything her colleagues had experienced. She spent days preparing—stringing up fairy lights, making sweets, and setting up her home to welcome her new friends into her world.
As the evening unfolded, her colleagues were captivated by the warmth and energy of the celebration. They marveled

at the brightly lit diyas, tasted the sweetness of gulab jamun for the first time, and swayed to the rhythmic beats of Bollywood music. Priya watched as the walls between her and her coworkers crumbled, replaced by genuine interest and admiration.

"I never knew much about Diwali before tonight," one of her colleagues said. "But I'm so glad you invited us. It feels like we've known you forever."

It wasn't just the food or the lights—it was the confidence Priya had found within herself. By inviting her colleagues into her world, she had allowed them to see her fully, and that vulnerability built a bridge. It was no longer just about polite exchanges or work-related interactions—it was about shared experiences, mutual respect, and deepening trust.

A New Perspective

By the end of her second year in Seattle, Priya had transformed—not just in the eyes of her colleagues, but in her own self-perception.

The truth was, her colleagues wanted to get to know her. They wanted her energy, her stories, and her perspective. But it was up to her to invite them in. In that way, Priya learned that building connections—whether personal or professional—wasn't just about fitting in; it was about standing out with confidence, authenticity, and curiosity.

* * *

Take Initiative, Speak up, and Be Bold

The core lesson of this chapter is simple: take initiative, speak up, and be bold. Engage with your colleagues in a way that breaks down barriers. Share your stories, inject humor, and connect on a personal level early on. Set aside formality and treat all your colleagues or clients as equals. These actions aren't just social skills—they're foundational to getting past the initial hurdles of forming relationships.

This chapter has laid the groundwork for building those initial connections. But remember in Western work culture, having a great personal connection, even a friendship, accounts for about 20% of your success. The other 80%? That's earned through your work—by proving yourself reliable, meeting deadlines, solving problems, and exceeding expectations.

The next chapter will explore how communication plays a pivotal role in building that trust. Miscommunication can unravel everything you've worked hard to build. We'll dive deep into how to ensure your message is clear, concise, and effective so you can thrive in any situation.

Skill 2: *Skip formalities and interact with new colleagues as if you've known them for years. Take the initiative instead of waiting for invitations. Break initial barriers with casual small talk, light-hearted humor, and conversations about shared interests or social activities. Once the connection is made, nurture the relationship naturally, just as you would back home.*

Exercise: The 5-Minute Common Interest Challenge

Objective: Build rapport with Western colleagues by discovering shared interests through small talk.

1. **Choose a Colleague Each Day:** Select a western colleague for a 5-minute chat during a natural break. Works both virtual or physical.

2. **Ask Open-Ended Questions:** Use questions like, "What do you enjoy doing on weekends?" or "Any hobbies outside of work?" to uncover possible shared interests discussed in this chapter.

3. **Listen for Common Ground:** If they mention something familiar, briefly share your experience or interest in it.

4. **Follow Up:** Ask one follow-up question to keep the conversation flowing, like "How did you get into that?"

5. **Reflect at Week's End:** Review what felt natural and note any shared interests for future connections.

Speak Your Mind: The Art of Clear, Honest Communication

❧❀❧

The importance of direct communication lies in avoiding speaking between the lines

When I first asked one of my Indian friends about communication in India, his response was revealing:

"Welcome to India—one word can have multiple meanings. The key is the context in which it's said."

For someone like me, coming from Norway and familiar with Western norms, this was quite the contrast. In the West, we often believe that *one word should only have one meaning*—context plays a role, but the meaning of what you're saying is usually found in the words themselves.

The difference between how words and context are used can lead to significant communication challenges, especially in professional environments where understanding is key.

Lost in Translation: The Subtle Signals That Go Unheard

Priya, an analyst based in India, was in a virtual meeting with Mark, her manager in the U.S. They were discussing a new project that required detailed data analysis and reporting.

As Mark explained the task, Priya was already feeling unsure about some of the technical aspects. After he finished, Priya hesitated but decided to say something.

"Okay, Mark. I think I understand most of it. I will try my best," she said, hoping her tone would signal that she wasn't fully confident.

Mark, however, took her words at face value. In his mind, "I will try my best" meant that Priya was fully on board and ready to tackle the task. "Great, Priya! Let me know if you run into any issues," he replied with a smile before ending the call.

Over the next few days, Priya struggled with the task. She didn't know exactly where to start, and the instructions weren't entirely clear. However, she didn't want to ask Mark for help directly, as she felt that might reflect poorly on her abilities. Instead, she sent him a polite message:

"Mark, I'm making some progress. I will send what I have by the end of the day."

To Mark, this sounded like everything was on track. He assumed she had it under control and didn't follow-up further.

When Priya finally submitted the report, it was completely off the mark. The analysis was not what Mark had asked for, and the results were incorrect. Frustrated, Mark sent her a message:

"Priya, this is not what we discussed. Did you understand the task? Why didn't you ask for help if you were struggling?"

Priya, feeling equally frustrated, thinking: "I did mention I wasn't sure and said I would try my best."

The miscommunication had left them both dissatisfied—Priya, because she felt her subtle hints were ignored, and Mark, because he thought she never asked for help. Neither realized that their different communication styles had caused the misunderstanding.

The story reflects a common scenario where communication is interpreted differently, leading to misunderstandings. One party believes they've conveyed their message clearly, while the other has interpreted it in an entirely different way. This confusion can have a big impact on work, especially in situations where negative feedback or difficult news needs to be communicated—like missing a deadline, struggling with a task, or disagreeing with a project decision.

You, as an Indian, might feel that you've expressed these concerns subtly, but there's a high chance your Western colleague has not understood the message. This is where the distinction between *high-context* communication, common in India, and *low-context* communication, typical in Western cultures, becomes crucial.

This chapter will explore how communication in the West differs from the Indian style and how you can bridge this gap. The goal is to help you understand and adapt to Western communication practices while staying within your comfort zone.

Low and High-Context Communication

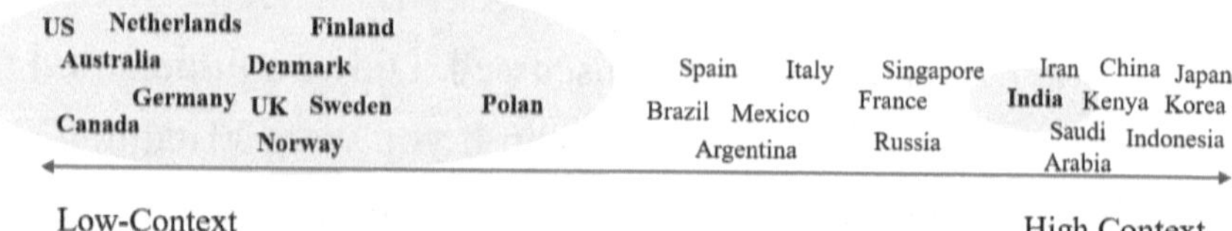

Figure 3.1 Communicating

Low Context: Good communication is precise, simple and clear. Messages are expressed and understood at face value. Repetition is appreciated if it help clarify the communication.

High context: Good communication is sophisticated, nuanced and layered. Messages are both spoken and read between the lines. Messages are often implied but not plainly expressed.

Source: Erin Meyer, *The culture map.*

Coming from a country that values low-context communication, compared to India's preference for high-context communication, I quickly realized how many misunderstandings might have occurred during my time in India. In low-context cultures like mine, messages are clear, direct, and detailed. People express their thoughts explicitly, with little left to interpretation. If a project is behind schedule, I'd say something like, *"The project is behind schedule. We need everyone to submit their parts by the end of the week to stay on track."* This leaves no room for ambiguity—both the problem and solution are clearly stated.

However, when I first started working in India, I noticed something that initially confused me. Deadlines seemed less urgent since no one was talking about them, no one appeared to be stressing or pushing for things to be done. At first, I thought my colleagues didn't care as much about timelines. But over time,

I realized they were indeed addressing these deadlines, just in a very different way.

In high-context communication, like in India, much of the meaning is conveyed through subtle cues, shared experiences, and unspoken signals. Words often serve as a starting point, while the true message lies between the lines. For example, in meetings, instead of directly saying, *"The project is delayed,"* a team leader might say, *"We hope everyone is considering the project timeline."* To me, this sounded vague. But to my Indian colleagues, it was a clear, polite reminder to pick up the pace—delivered in a way that aligns with their cultural norms.

Reflecting on these moments, I realized the misunderstanding wasn't due to a lack of urgency, but rather to our different communication styles. I hadn't recognized the subtleties in their high-context communication. While I was waiting for someone to explicitly mention a problem, they were already addressing it in their own, indirect way.

These examples show how, in high-context cultures like India, communication relies on implicit meanings and suggestions. Listeners are expected to pick up on these cues and understand what's being implied. On the other hand, in low-context cultures, like those in the West, communication is more explicit and focused on clarity, minimizing the risk of misunderstandings by stating everything plainly.

The figure below is the key concepts that we are going to discuss in this chapter. The chapter will first focus on cultural differences before we move over to how to overcome them.

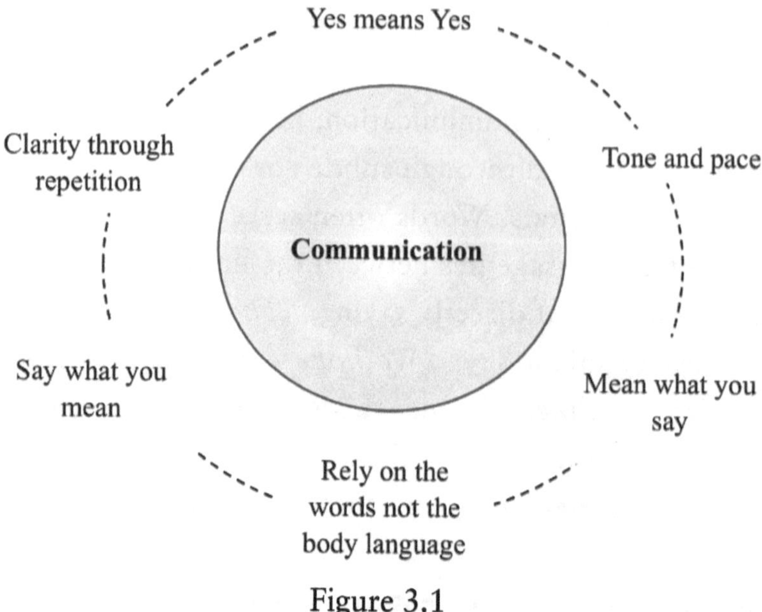

Figure 3.1

Cross-Cultural Communication Gaps

Bustling office in Bangalore

In a bustling office in Bangalore, Priya, the project leader of a multinational software development team, prepared for her video call with John, the project manager based in New York. The project was high-stakes, involving critical software updates for a global client, and the deadline was fast approaching.

> **Priya:** (connecting the call) "Good evening, John. I hope your morning is off to a good start."
>
> **John:** "Good evening, Priya. Yes, thanks. Let's dive in—how are we progressing with the project updates?"
>
> **Priya:** "We've been carefully reviewing the modules. There are some intricate aspects that require detailed attention. We're ensuring everything meets the highest standards."

John: "Sounds good. So, are we still on track for the April 30th delivery?"

Priya: "As you know, quality is the top priority. We're aligning our resources to make sure everything meets expectations. It's important each phase gets the focus it needs."

John: "Absolutely, quality is critical. But we also need to hit our deadline. Do you need more resources? Are there areas where you foresee delays?"

Priya: "The team is working around the clock, and we're balancing priorities. Given the complexities, some areas might need further refinement."

John: "Okay, but are we on track for the deadline? Should I take it that we're managing within the time frame?"

Priya: "Yes, the team is committed. We're doing our best to meet the timeline."

The call ended with John reassured that things were on schedule, while Priya was left worried but hesitant to contradict the deadline outright. Weeks passed, and as the deadline loomed, several critical components of the software were still incomplete.

John: (in a follow-up call, frustrated) "Priya, we're a week away from the deadline, and I just heard from the team that some key features aren't ready. Why am I finding this out now?"

Priya: "John, I mentioned in our last call that ensuring quality might stretch our capacity. We've been facing unexpected challenges that have slowed our progress."

John: "But you never directly said we were at risk of missing the deadline. I thought we were just dealing with normal project hurdles. Why wasn't this communicated clearly?"

Priya: "I tried to convey that we were under pressure and that timelines might be tight given our focus on quality..."

John: "I needed a clear answer—either we're on track or we're not. Now we're in a tough spot with our client."

In this scenario, the miscommunication between Priya and John wasn't due to a lack of effort but rather a difference in communication styles. Priya's indirect, high-context communication didn't clearly signal the urgency of the situation, while John's low-context approach expected directness. This cultural gap led to frustration on both sides and a risk to their client relationship.

Differences in Communication Styles

Priya's High-Context Approach: When Priya she mentioned 'intricate aspects' and the need for 'meticulous attention to detail,' she was subtly hinting at possible delays. Her comments about aligning resources and focusing on quality were meant to signal that the project might fall behind schedule.

John's Low-Context Expectations: John, on the other hand, was accustomed to a low-context communication style, where direct and explicit statements are the norm. He interpreted Priya's words as reassurance about the project's quality, not as a warning about potential delays. What John needed was a clear statement like, "We're behind schedule" or "We need more resources." In fact, to be sure her message got through, Priya would have benefited from repeating the point several times. In Western cultures, clarity and repetition help ensure everyone's on the same page.

Expectations of Implicit Understanding

- **Priya's Expectations:** Priya may have expected John to pick up on her hints about the project challenges. In high-context communication, much of the meaning is conveyed implicitly, relying on the other person to read between the lines.

- **John's Literal Interpretation:** But John, without experience in high-context communication, took Priya's updates at face value. He believed that while there were challenges, they were under control and wouldn't impact the timeline, since they were not explicitly mentioned.

Remember this - both Priya and John were communicating in ways that made sense within their own cultural frameworks, but their messages were lost in translation.

Reflection point: Have you ever been in a situation where you did not feel heard or understood by your Western colleagues?

Body Language

One of my former colleagues, Vatsal, once told me how crucial body language is in India. He explained that when you're talking to someone, it's not just the words that matter—you have to look at the entire picture. The body language of the person you're speaking to is just as important as what they say. As Rohan, another colleague, once told me, the message has to be interpreted in the full context of how it's delivered. The problem is, as a Westerner, this isn't how I—and most people from the West—communicate. We rely on words to be clear and direct, especially at work. Sure, we use body language, but it's secondary to what's actually said.

This difference creates a huge potential for misunderstandings. In Western cultures, we don't rely much on non-verbal cues like tone of voice, facial expressions, or gestures to convey meaning. Yes, body language exists here, and if you're good at reading it, it can definitely give you an edge. But be cautious. Western body language isn't always interpreted the same way as it is in India. If you try to read the body language of a Western colleague based on your Indian cultural understanding, you might completely misinterpret what's going on—and that's where the trouble starts.

It all makes sense when you think about it. Every country, just like every household, has its own unique way of communicating. Growing up with my sister, mum, and dad, I learned to read their body language. I could look at my sister and immediately tell if she needed space, or at my mum and know if she was happy, sad, or stressed. That's because we lived together, and over time, I learned to read their cues. But if someone from outside our family visited, they wouldn't pick up on those same signals the way I did. They might completely miss the little tells that I took for granted.

The same thing happens when we step into another culture. India is like a new 'house' for someone from the West, just as the a Western country is for someone from India. We don't naturally understand the subtle non-verbal cues that locals do, and if we try to interpret them based on our own cultural framework, we risk getting it all wrong. Take something as simple as nodding in

India, for example. There are so many ways to nod, and each one can mean something different. After spending just a few months in India, I found myself picking up the head nods, though I have no idea if I did it right. I probably confused people by shaking my head all the time! But in Western countries, nodding is simple—up and down means 'yes', and side to side means 'no'. That's not the case in India, and even now, I still get confused about what means what.

Yes Problem

The 'Yes' Problem

Reflection point: Before starting to read the section below, take a moment to reflect on what the "yes" problem might refer to.

After reflecting you might have heard of the 'yes' problem. Either way, it's something worth discussing, as it's one of the central aspects of understanding differences in communication that often puzzle people from Western countries.

The word 'yes' can have different meanings in Western countries compared to India. When I say 'yes', I mean it unequivocally—'yes' means 'yes', not 'no', not 'maybe', not 'I'm not sure', or 'please explain further'. It simply means 'yes'. For example, if someone asks me if I understand a question and I do, I say 'yes'. If I don't understand, I'll say, "I don't understand, please explain more." Or if someone asks if

their work was good and I think it wasn't, I'll say "no." If the work was good, of course, I'll say "yes."

You might see where I'm going with this. Having lived in India and worked with people from India for several years, I've learned that this straightforward use of 'yes' and 'no' differs in India, especially in certain contexts. Among close friends, Indians might use 'yes' and 'no' more directly, but in the early stages of a relationship, in a work setting, or when dealing with someone higher up in the hierarchy, these words can become harder to use. This stems from various cultural factors, which will be explored throughout this book. But we're addressing it here because it closely relates to high-context versus low-context communication.

What I've learned is that you as an Indian do say 'yes' and 'no', but they might not always use these words directly. Instead, the meaning is conveyed through the situation, context, and body language. The challenge arises because Westerners often don't pick up on these subtleties. They need to hear 'yes' when that's the intended meaning, and 'no' when that's what's being implied. You can believe that by not saying yes you prioritize maintaining harmony, but here's the key: even if you say, "No, I don't understand, please explain it to me again," instead of saying 'yes, I understand', harmony remains intact. In fact, it's quite the opposite—the person you're working with will appreciate your honesty in expressing that you need further clarification early on. If you say "yes", but in reality, you mean maybe or no, that person will lose trust in you.

Let's revisit a section from the story earlier in this chapter about John and Priya.

John: "Okay, but are we on track for the deadline? Should I assume that we're managing within the timeframe?"

Priya: "Yes, the team is committed. We're doing our best to meet the timeline."

As the story reflects, misunderstandings can easily arise. Priya believed her message was clearly understood, but John needed to hear the explicit words, **"No, we are not meeting the deadline,"** to fully understand the situation and take the necessary actions. Without this clear statement, he assumed everything was on track, leading to frustration and potential project risks.

Repetition, Repetition, Repetition

Repetition, repetition, repetition—if there's one thing you need to know about communication with Westerners, it's that we love repetition. Just yesterday, I sat through a meeting where, as usual, we began with a detailed agenda that laid out every point we'd cover. We meticulously followed this agenda, avoiding any deviations (but more on that in the chapter about time). And, of course, by the end of the meeting, we recapped all the key points, making sure nothing was left ambiguous. Finally, an email followed, summarizing everything: *"Thanks for the meeting, everyone. Just to recap, Jon, you're handling X, and Jenny, you've got Y. If anything is unclear, please reach out immediately."*

Westerners, particularly in business settings, thrive on structure. We like to start with a clear agenda, outline each topic in detail, and wrap up with a summary of the key points and decisions. Tasks are clearly assigned to specific individuals, with deadlines that are explicitly stated. This method minimizes the risk of misunderstandings and ensures that everyone is on the same page about what needs to be done.

What does this tell us? In Western countries, repetition isn't just a preference—it's essential for effective communication. Without it, misunderstandings are almost guaranteed. Westerners depend on clear, repeated summaries and explicit task assignments to ensure that everyone is aligned and fully aware of their responsibilities.

Reflection point: Do you use the power of repetition in your work today?

Bridging The Communication Gap

R-E-S-P-E-C-T Framework

So, what does it take to communicate effectively in the West? It all boils down to seven key elements that, when mastered, can give you a significant advantage. These seven principles, when combined, can be summed up by one word:

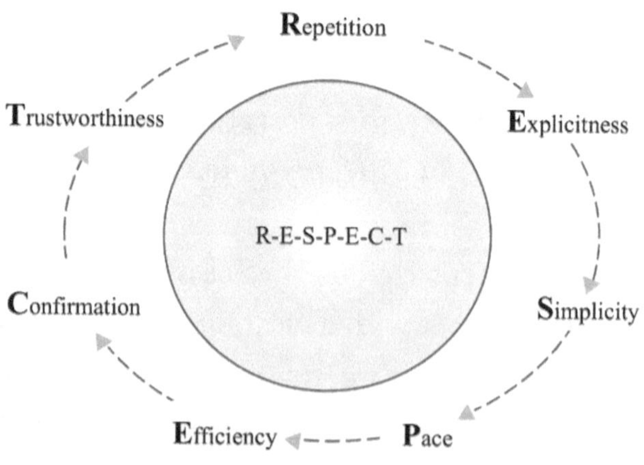

Figure 3.2

Here's how it breaks down:

R – Repetition

Repetition is essential to reinforce your message, ensuring it sticks and is fully understood.

E – Explicitness

Being explicit means communicating clearly and directly, leaving no room for misunderstanding or ambiguity.

S – Simplicity

Simplicity ensures that your ideas are straightforward and accessible, helping to avoid confusion.

P – Pace

Pace refers to the rhythm of communication—balancing speed so that the conversation flows naturally without feeling rushed or dragging.

E – Efficiency

Efficiency is about optimizing communication for time and impact. It's all about keeping it concise without sacrificing meaning.

C – Confirmation

Always seek confirmation that your message has been understood. This not only avoids misunderstandings but also shows that you care about clarity.

T – Trustworthiness

Communication grounded in trust is built on honesty and integrity. Trust ensures that what you say will be taken seriously. Don't say yes unless you truly mean yes.

As we move through this chapter, we will explore each of these elements in detail, breaking down the barriers and strategies that will help you master communication in western settings.

Communication scale

What might be seen as effective and clear communication in the West can often be perceived as impersonal or even rude in India. Let's dive deeper into this with a cultural scale that highlights the differences between **direct** (low-context) and **indirect** (high-context) communication styles.

India	Indirect	Direct	Bold	n/a
West	n/a	Indirect	Direct	Bold

Figure 3.3

Source: Craig Story, "speaking of India"

As you can see, what might be considered rude or bold in India is actually seen as direct, efficient, and clear communication in the West. On the flip side, when Indians aim to be direct, it can often come across as indirect to Westerners. The result? Misunderstandings. Why? Because when Indians are direct or indirect it often falls outside the spectrum of what Westerners are familiar with—so far outside, in fact, that the intended message can be completely lost.

In the following pages, we'll dive into strategies that will help you navigate and overcome these communication challenges. You'll discover that, from your perspective, you may need to push the boundaries of what feels 'on the edge of rudeness' to communicate effectively with your Western colleagues. And trust me, we will appreciate that directness every step of the way because you pushing yourself to being bold is just normal communication for us.

Be 'bold', be direct, say your opinion regardless of who you talk to.

S – Simplicity and E - Explicitness

Simplicity ensures that your ideas are straightforward and accessible, helping to avoid confusion.

Let's take a look at two different communication style scenarios.

Scenario 1: Indian Communication Style

Raj: "Good morning, Priya. I wanted to discuss the project report you submitted yesterday. You've put in a lot of effort, and I appreciate that."

Priya: "Good morning, Raj. Thank you! I'm happy to discuss it. Does it cover everything we need?"

Raj: "It's thorough, but I'm thinking that maybe we could fine-tune some of the analysis sections, look over grammar and the logical structure. You know how management is—they appreciate a little extra detail."

Priya: "Absolutely. I'll go through the report again and make those improvements. Do you need it by the end of the day?"

Raj: "That would be great if you can manage. No rush, but it would help us keep things on track. Thanks for taking this on."

In this example, Raj uses indirect language to hint at the need for revisions without explicitly stating that there's a problem. Priya's offer to revise the report by the end of the day is polite but vague, and Raj's casual mention of 'no rush' reflects the high-context communication style often found in Indian culture. This can lead to delays when working with Western colleagues, who expect clear deadlines and direct requests.

Scenario 2: Western Communication Style

John: "Morning, Lisa. I've gone through the report you submitted. Thanks for getting it to me on time. However, the analysis section is too broad, and I can't pinpoint clear conclusions. In addition, there are a few sentences that lack logical structure, and I have found five grammatical errors. It's not ready for the management review."

Lisa: "Got it, John. So to narrow down exactly what needs to be fixed. I should add more data, tighten the conclusions and send it for both a grammatical and logical check? Agree?"

John: "Yes, I agree. We need clearer conclusions, more supporting data, and any sort of logical or grammatical issues will take the focus away from the real value of the report, so must be fixed. Can you have it revised and ready by 5 PM today? It's important we stay on track for tomorrow's review meeting."

Lisa: "Understood. I'll get it done by 5 pm and let you know if I run into any roadblocks."

John: "Good."

In this Western context, John is direct, clearly highlighting the issues with the report and setting a firm deadline. Lisa responds by asking for specific feedback and commits to the deadline, ensuring no misunderstandings. This type of communication leaves little room for doubt, which is typical in low-context, direct cultures like the U.S., where clarity and efficiency are highly valued. The primary meaning is conveyed through words, with no need for interpretation or guesswork.

What makes this topic hard but very important is that what might seem like a clear and polite statement to an Indian speaker can leave a Westerner scratching their head, unsure of the true meaning. To bridge this gap, we will explore how indirect phrases can be interpreted differently across cultures.

Let's look at some examples of common indirect phrases used in India, which can often lead to confusion for Westerners:

Example 1: 'We will see how things go.'

- **How it's understood in India:** This is a way of saying, "We'll evaluate the situation as it develops and adapt." It's a flexible and cautious approach, signaling that a decision will be made based on evolving circumstances.
- **How it's interpreted in the West:** A Westerner might hear this and think that there's no clear plan or commitment. To them, it could come across as indecision or an unwillingness to take concrete action.

Example 2: 'We should be able to meet the deadline.'
- **How it's understood in India:** This is a polite way of suggesting that there may be challenges with meeting the deadline, but the speaker doesn't want to say it outright. It's an indirect hint that things may not be on track.
- **How it's interpreted in the West:** Westerners often take this as a confirmation that the deadline will be met, with just a slight possibility of delay. They may not pick up on the subtle caution embedded in the phrase.

Example 3: 'The project is progressing.'
- **How it's understood in India:** This phrase can be a way of saying that while the project is moving forward, there are likely issues that are slowing things down. It's a softer way of addressing problems without openly stating them.

- **How it's interpreted in the West:** For a Westerner, this may signal that everything is going well and on schedule. The indirect hint that there are challenges may go unnoticed, leading to false confidence in the project's status.

Example 4: 'I'll try my best.'
- **How it's understood in India:** This phrase is often used as a polite way of saying, "I'll attempt to do this, but it might not be possible." It's a way of avoiding saying 'no' directly while still acknowledging the difficulty.
- **How it's interpreted in the West:** Westerners tend to hear this as a solid commitment to getting the task done. The nuance of uncertainty can be lost, leading them to believe the task will be completed without issue.

As you can see, what seems like a straightforward statement in one culture can have multiple layers of meaning in another. For Westerners, clear and direct communication is often expected, whereas in India, subtlety and indirectness are valued to maintain harmony and avoid confrontation. This is why it's crucial to recognize these differences, as they can easily lead to misunderstandings if left unaddressed. Being explicit in your communication leaves no room for interpretation beyond your actual words—exactly the clarity we're aiming to achieve.

Below are some specific tips and examples to help clarify your messages and simplify your language when working with Western colleagues. These strategies will help you shift toward a more direct communication style, ensuring that your ideas are understood without ambiguity.

Use Specific and Action-Oriented Verbs
- *Indirect:* "We might consider sending the report by next week."
- *Direct:* "Please send the report by next Wednesday."

Avoid Qualifiers That Weaken Statements
- Qualifiers like 'just', 'maybe', 'perhaps', or 'kind of' can dilute the strength of your message.

- *Indirect:* "I just wanted to suggest that we could try a new approach."
- *Direct:* "Let's try a new approach."

Use Time-Specific Language
- Instead of using vague timelines, give precise dates and times.
- *Indirect:* "We should complete the project soon."
- *Direct:* "We need to complete the project by October 5th."

Avoid Ambiguity in Responses
- Be clear in your affirmations or disagreements.
- *Indirect:* "Yes, but it might need some changes."
- *Direct:* "Yes, I agree, but let's revise the budget section specifically."

Use Simple Language
- Avoid jargon and complex vocabulary that might confuse the listener.
- *Indirect:* "We anticipate a felicitous outcome from this synergistic approach."
- *Direct:* "We expect good results from this team effort."

R- Repetition and C - Confirmation

Repetition is essential to reinforce your message, ensuring it sticks and is fully understood.

Always seek confirmation that your message has been understood. This not only avoids misunderstandings but also shows that you care about clarity.

In every meeting I've had—whether with colleagues in the U.S., France, the Netherlands, or Germany—the process follows a familiar pattern: we start with a clear agenda, discuss the key points, and wrap up with a summary. This ensures everyone leaves with a 100% understanding of the next steps. In Western cultures, repetition is crucial for reinforcing messages and ensuring alignment. If you leave a meeting without confirming or repeating what was discussed, you're signaling that you fully understood—and from that point, the expectation is that you'll deliver flawlessly.

Five Tips for Summarizing and Confirming After Meetings

Here are five practical tips to ensure clarity and avoid misunderstandings when summarizing and confirming agreements after meetings:

1. ***Summarize Key Points Clearly***

   - *Tip:* Recap the main topics, decisions, and insights at the end of each meeting to reinforce what was discussed.
   - *Example:* "To summarize, the next steps are A, B, and C. Team X will handle client follow-up by next Wednesday."

2. ***Allocate Tasks Explicitly***

   - *Tip:* Clearly assign responsibilities to prevent confusion and ensure accountability.
   - *Example:* "Raj will finalize the budget by Friday, and Priya will prepare the presentation for Monday."

3. ***Confirm Understanding and Commitment***

   - *Tip:* Ask team members to confirm their tasks and deadlines to avoid any misunderstandings.
   - *Example:* "Anil, I am handling the data analysis, correct? This will be done by Thursday?"

4. ***Use Reflective Listening***

   - *Tip:* Echo key points to confirm your understanding and show engagement.

- *Example:* "So, if I understand correctly, next week's focus is on logistics, and Sita will lead coordination. Is that right?"

5. ***End with a Call for Questions***

- *Tip:* Encourage questions to ensure clarity and prevent unresolved doubts.
- *Example:* "Before we close, does anyone have any questions or need further clarification on today's tasks?"

E – Efficiency

Efficiency is about optimizing communication for time and impact. It's all about keeping it concise without sacrificing meaning – in short: get to the point.

Western business communication often follows a linear, logical structure. I like to explain it through two metaphors: the linear structure of Western communication as a train and the more fluid style seen in Indian contexts as a river.

In Western communication, like a train, the approach is direct and follows a fixed track. Messages are delivered with precision, moving from point A to point B without deviation. There's a clear beginning, middle, and end, all focused on efficiency and getting to the conclusion on time.

On the other hand, Indian communication is more like a river. It flows freely, often meandering through various topics, allowing for a broader context and a more holistic view. Discussions may circle around and explore tangents before coming to a conclusion, contributing to a deeper understanding, even if it takes longer to get there.

Adopting and mastering a more structured, linear communication style can significantly improve your interactions with Western colleagues. Below are practical tips and examples to help you align with the norms of Western business communication.

1. **Set a Clear Agenda** Before any meeting, always prepare an agenda outlining each topic with specific time slots. This helps keep the discussion focused and ensures that all key points are addressed efficiently. While you don't need to share the time slots with others, having them keeps you aware of how efficiently you need to manage each discussion point.

2. **Start with the End in Mind** Begin all communications, whether it's an email or a meeting, by clearly stating the objective. This sets expectations and directs the conversation toward achieving specific outcomes.
    Example: In an email to a client: "The goal of our upcoming meeting is to finalize the key milestones for the Q4 project so we can allocate resources and meet the deadlines efficiently."

3. **Follow a Structured Approach in Meetings** Use the agenda to guide the meeting, addressing each point in order. Begin with a review of the last meeting's key takeaways, follow with a progress update, and conclude by discussing next steps.

4. **Emphasize Key Points** Highlight the main ideas at the start and end of your communications to reinforce key takeaways. In presentations, for instance, use summary slides at the beginning and end to emphasize crucial points.

5. **Limit Tangential Discussions** While diverse perspectives are valuable, steer conversations back to the agenda when they stray. You might say something like:

Example 2: "These are interesting points. To make the best use of our time, let's return to our main topic. We can schedule another session to explore these ideas further."

6. **Use Bullet Points for Clarity** Organize your information in bullet points, whether in emails or presentations, to convey messages clearly and succinctly.

7. **Practice Time Management** Respect the time allocated for each agenda item to ensure all points are covered without rushing through important topics.

You can visit larshelgesen.com to download samples of agendas, emails, and more as templates for communicating with your Western counterparts.

P - Pace

Pace refers to the rhythm of communication—balancing speed so that the conversation flows naturally without feeling rushed or dragging.

I'll admit, the first time I had a video call with an Indian colleague, I struggled to fully grasp what was being said. From the range of words used to the pace of speaking, I found myself a bit lost. After the conversation ended, I realized I hadn't understood the whole picture. Since it was just a feedback session and not directly related to work, I didn't push for clarification, thinking it was an issue with my own English comprehension. However, as time passed—and after speaking with colleagues who shared similar experiences—I realized it wasn't just me. Many of my fellow Western colleagues have mentioned that they often catch only half of what's being said in these conversations. But why is this happening when we're all speaking English?

I know Indian professionals speak excellent English, often better than many of my colleagues here in Norway. So, where's the disconnect? After spending time trying to pinpoint the issue, I've identified three key areas where these communication barriers arise: Accent and Pronunciation, Vocabulary and Idioms, Speed, and Intonation.

Accent and Pronunciation:

- Indian English often carries a distinct accent, influenced by your native languages, which can be difficult for Westerners who are unfamiliar with these patterns.

Vocabulary and Idioms:

- Indian English includes unique words and expressions that may be unfamiliar to Western ears. For example, terms like 'prepone' (rescheduling to an earlier time) and 'hill station' (a town in the hills) aren't common in Western English.

Speed and Intonation:

- The speed at which you speak and the intonation patterns can differ greatly. You may speak faster, or place emphasis on different parts of the sentence, which can make it harder for a Western listener to follow the conversation.

Understanding these differences is the first step toward improving communication. It's important to note that if you're unsure whether your message was understood, don't hesitate to ask for confirmation or offer a clearer explanation. The best advice I can give is to encourage open dialogue. Let your counterpart know it's okay to ask for clarification, and do the same when you're unsure.

Here are some practical tips to make sure your message comes across clearly:

1. **Keep Your Tone Even**: Speak with a steady tone, and avoid ending sentences as though you're asking a question unless you truly are. This keeps your points clear and reduces the chance of confusion.

2. **Practice Common Business Words**: Work on pronouncing key business terms clearly. Listening to native speakers and repeating these words aloud can help make your pronunciation easy to follow.

3. **Use Familiar Words**: Substitute unique Indian English terms like "prepone" with words Western colleagues know, such as "reschedule." This keeps your message straightforward and clear.

4. **Slow Your Pace**: Speak a bit slower than usual to allow listeners time to process each word. A calm pace makes it easier for them to follow along.

5. **Emphasize Key Words**: Place extra emphasis on main words in your sentences, like nouns and verbs. For example, instead of saying "We can finish the report by tomorrow," try "We can finish the **report** by **tomorrow**," so the most important points are clear.

6. **Check for Clarity**: After conversations, simply ask if everything was clear. This helps you improve continuously and shows that you value being understood.

These small adjustments will help make your communication more direct, ensuring your message is understood and appreciated by Western colleagues.

T – Trustworthiness

Communication grounded in trust is built on honesty and integrity. Trust ensures that what you say will be taken seriously. Don't say yes unless you truly mean yes.

One of the more interesting cultural differences I encountered early on was how people provide information, particularly when they don't have the full answer. At first, I thought this was just a quirk of individual behavior—perhaps even a sign that someone was trying to mislead me. But the more time I spent in India, the more I realized it was something far deeper and more ingrained in the culture.

Let me share an experience that stands out vividly from my early days in Mumbai. Picture this: I was new to the city, in the streets, trying to find my way to the Phoenix Palladium—a large shopping center where I hoped to find Wi-Fi, as I hadn't yet sorted out a local SIM card. It was scorching hot, nearly 40 degrees Celsius, and I was starting to feel a little desperate. No phone, no Wi-Fi, no way to contact anyone. So, I turned to the good old-fashioned method of asking for directions.

I spotted a man on the street and approached him. He looked a little surprised when I asked how to get to the Palladium, but with a friendly smile, he pointed to the left and said, "Walk five minutes." Relieved, I set off in that direction, but after ten minutes of walking, I still wasn't anywhere near the shopping center. Starting to feel the heat—and the frustration—I decided to ask a group of schoolchildren who seemed approachable. To my dismay, they pointed me right back to where I had started.

Now, I was well and truly lost, wandering the crowded streets of one of the largest cities in the world, with no clue where to go. Hungry, overheated, and a little exasperated, I remembered the advice my colleagues had given me: "If in doubt, get a cab." Surely, the cab drivers would know the way. I flagged one down and told him I needed to go to Phoenix Palladium. He gestured for me to hop in, and off we went. After what felt like an eternity—but in reality, was about 35 minutes—I finally spotted the familiar sign for the Palladium.

This was my first real experience with how people in India handle giving information. The man on the street, the children, even the cab driver—they all wanted to be helpful, even though not all of them actually knew the right answer. And that's the key. In Indian culture, there's a deep-rooted desire to maintain social harmony, to be polite, and to avoid the awkwardness of saying, "I don't know." This leads to people giving directions or advice with the best intentions, even when they're not entirely sure.

To someone like me, coming from a Western background, this was a bit of a shock. In Western cultures, there's no shame in admitting you don't know something—in fact, it's often seen as a mark of honesty. We value directness and accuracy over the need to avoid discomfort or save face. This difference in approach can cause confusion if you're not aware of it.

But here's the beauty of it: once I understood the cultural context, everything made sense. In India, the goal is to be helpful, even if that means improvising a bit. In contrast, Westerners often prioritize precision, even if that means saying, "I don't know."

Understanding this difference is crucial if you're looking to improve communication across cultures. While confidence in your communication is important, it needs to be balanced with accuracy. Overconfidence, especially when it's not backed by solid information, can lead to mistakes and misunderstandings.

So, as much as it's about being polite, it's also about finding that balance—being helpful while ensuring you're giving the right information.

To bridge this cultural gap and enhance your communication with Western colleagues, there are a few strategies you can adopt that better align with their expectations. Here are some practical approaches, along with examples, to help navigate these differences effectively:

Admit When You Don't Know

- In Western cultures, honesty and directness are appreciated. Admitting when you don't know something is seen as a strength rather than a weakness.
- **Example:** If someone asks for directions and you're unsure, say, "I'm not exactly sure of the way, but it might be a good idea to check with someone else or use a map."
- **Practice:** Get comfortable with phrases like "I don't know," "I'm not sure," or "Let me find out for you." This not only prevents miscommunication but also builds trust.

Understand and Respect Direct Communication.

- Westerners value direct communication as a sign of respect and efficiency. Adopting a straightforward approach will greatly improve mutual understanding.
- **Example:** If you can't help immediately, be direct: "I'm sorry, I can't assist with that right now, but I'll find out and get back to you as soon as possible."
- **Practice:** Be clear and concise in your responses. Avoid overcomplicating the message. This will reduce misunderstandings and better align with Western communication styles.

Balance Confidence with Accuracy.

- Confidence is important, but it must be matched with accuracy. Overconfidence without solid information can hurt your credibility and lead to mistakes. The problem arises if you commit to something by saying "yes" and you fail to fulfill that commitment you set yourselves up for failure.

- **Example:** Instead of saying, "We'll definitely finish by Friday," say, "Based on our current progress, we aim to finish by Friday, but I'll update you if anything changes."
- **Practice:** Regularly review and double-check your work before making confident statements. Seeking feedback from colleagues to ensure your information is accurate will strengthen your professional reliability.

'No stupid questions'

Reflection point: Use two minutes to reflect on what you think is meant by "no stupid questions", is this a term you are familiar with?

What brings the R-E-S-P-E-C-T framework together is the value of open dialogue. You might be familiar with the phrase, "There are no stupid questions." While this idea might exist in Indian workplaces, in Western cultures, it's a fundamental aspect of communication—from school to the boardroom. Asking questions isn't just accepted; it's expected. It's seen as a way to ensure efficiency and clarity, so if you're ever unsure about something, don't hesitate. Seek help instead of wasting time trying to figure it out on your own.

Of course, this doesn't mean asking constant questions without trying to solve the issue yourself. The key is balance—try to figure it out first, but if you're stuck for more than an hour or two, don't be afraid to ask for guidance. In Western workplaces, this kind of approach promotes a collaborative atmosphere where everyone feels comfortable seeking clarification, which leads to a more productive team.

In the West, questions are viewed as a way to gain a better understanding, not as a challenge or a sign of incompetence. For example, if you ask, "Can you explain why we chose this approach?" it's taken as a genuine attempt to understand, not as questioning authority. **If you avoid asking questions, your Western colleagues might assume you fully understand everything, which can lead to confusion or mistakes.**

So, remember—asking questions is seen as a positive and necessary part of communication. It shows you're engaged, proactive, and committed to getting the work done right.

Here are a few tips to help you effectively adopt this approach:

Understand the Value of Questions

Insight: In Western cultures, asking questions shows engagement and a willingness to learn. It demonstrates that you're proactive and committed to understanding your work. In India, comprehensive introductions are often the norm, but in the West, introductions tend to be brief, leaving it up to you to fully understand the context by asking relevant questions.

Example: If you're unclear about a task, asking for clarification can help prevent mistakes and show that you care about delivering quality work.

Create a Safe Space for Yourself

Tip: Remind yourself that asking questions is valuable and valid. Practice saying phrases like, "I need some clarification on this," to build your confidence.

Example: During a meeting, if something isn't clear, say, "Could you explain that point again? I want to make sure I fully understand."

Prepare Questions in Advance

Tip: Write down your questions before a meeting to make sure you don't forget them and can articulate them clearly. You might even consider sending them to participants beforehand so they can prepare detailed answers. After formulating your questions, take the time to develop hypotheses about what the answers might be.

Example: Before a project meeting, draft your questions and email them to the team, saying, "I've prepared a few questions for our meeting to ensure I fully understand the project requirements."

❖ ❖ ❖

Speak up, share your opinions, and make your voice heard

Bringing it all together, we have the word RESPECT—a framework designed to help you, as an Indian professional, communicate in a way that Western colleagues truly understand. That's the goal of this chapter, and as a Westerner who values clarity through repetition, I've reinforced this theme throughout. The aim is to help you convey exactly what you mean, with confidence and precision, in every interaction. Let's summarize the RESPECT framework.

First, **Repetition** is not just a courtesy but a necessity in Western communication. Summarizing key points, confirming understanding, and repeating important deadlines or tasks help to reinforce your message. In many cases, repetition ensures that everyone leaves a meeting or conversation with complete clarity, without any room for misunderstanding.

Next comes **Explicitness**. Being direct is crucial. In Western contexts, there's little room for reading between the lines. You need to say exactly what you mean, whether it's giving feedback, setting expectations, or even admitting when you don't know something. This isn't seen as confrontational—it's about being honest and avoiding ambiguity. **Simplicity** is tied closely to this, as clear, straightforward language helps others understand your point quickly. Strip away any unnecessary complexity and focus on delivering your message concisely.

Pace refers to the rhythm of communication—balancing speed so that conversations flow naturally without feeling rushed or dragged out. Given the variety of accents and dialects, it's often better to speak slowly and ensure your message is understood, rather than rushing through and risking confusion.

Efficiency is key in structuring your communication. Westerners value time, so getting straight to the point without unnecessary background is appreciated. A **linear communication style**—with a clear beginning, middle, and end—helps maintain focus and ensures that discussions are productive.

Confirmation is about ensuring that your message has landed as intended. Western colleagues will often expect you to explicitly confirm your understanding or clarify if you have any doubts. Failing to do so can signal that you've understood everything perfectly, even if that's not the case. This is where asking questions is not only acceptable but encouraged, tying into the principle that 'there are no stupid questions.'

Finally, **Trustworthiness**—which comes from honesty and integrity—is at the heart of effective communication. When you are open, direct, and clear in your interactions, you build trust. Westerners appreciate honesty, even if it means admitting uncertainty or requesting more information. Trust is built through consistent communication where your words and actions align.

As you move forward, there's one crucial thing you must embrace and remember: step out of your comfort zone, speak up, share your opinions, and make your voice heard. Sticking to the old Indian traditions of maintaining harmony, saving face, and respecting hierarchy will not serve you—it will hold you back. Those traits may be essential for success in India but will cause you to fail in the West. To thrive, you need to break free from those values and embrace directness, openness, and gain the confidence to challenge.

As we wrap up our communication, it's essential to recognize that how we communicate is deeply intertwined with how we manage our time. Clear, concise, and direct communication isn't just about ensuring understanding—it's about respecting everyone's time, eliminating unnecessary delays, and ensuring that actions follow swiftly. In the West, time isn't just a tool; it's a precious resource that drives every decision, deadline, and interaction. In the next chapter, you'll learn how to master efficiency and punctuality, helping you align with Western expectations. Ready to make every minute count?

Skill 3: *Master Clear, Honest Communication and Embrace Constructive Feedback; Understand the importance of saying what you mean and mean what you say. Embrace simplicity and clarity in your words without using body language or indirect meanings.*

Exercise: *Direct Yes/No Challenge*

Objective: Practice clear responses by confidently saying "yes" or "no" to ensure transparent communication.

1. **Identify One Daily Situation:** Each day, choose one situation where you're asked for a commitment, deadline, or decision—something you might normally respond to indirectly.
2. **Respond Clearly and Honestly:** Practice a straightforward response based on your true capacity:
   - **Yes:** "Yes, I can complete this by [date]."
   - **No:** "No, I won't be able to do this right now." Or " No, I need more guidance".
3. **Avoid Buffer Words:** Eliminate phrases like "I'll try," "maybe," or "I'll see" to keep your response clear and direct.
4. **Provide a Brief Alternative if Needed:** If saying "no," suggest a realistic alternative, like "I can't finish by Friday, but I can complete it by Monday."
5. **End with Confirmation:** If saying "yes," end with a confirmation phrase, like "Does this timeline work for you?" or "Let me know if this aligns with your needs."

4

Time is Money: How to Maximize Every Moment

❧✳❧

Adapting to the Western view of time and boosting workplace efficiency

In the West, time is money – spend it well

Time is a curious thing. While the ticking of a clock is the same for everyone, the way we experience those ticks is deeply personal, shaped by our backgrounds, emotions, and the culture we're part of. The clock might offer a universal measure, but how we feel time passing is anything but universal.

For some, time flies when they're fully engaged in something they enjoy. Whether it's working on a project you're passionate about or spending time with loved ones, hours can slip by in what feels like minutes. This is what psychologists call 'flow' – a state where time becomes fluid, and we lose ourselves in the moment.

On the other hand, time can drag, especially when we're stressed, bored, or waiting for something important. Ever been stuck in a long meeting or anxiously waiting for important news? In those moments, every minute can feel like an eternity. It's proof that time isn't just something we measure, but something we feel, and that feeling can shift dramatically depending on our circumstances.

Cultural perspectives also shape how we view time. In many Western countries, time is closely tied to productivity. The phrase "time is money" reflects this idea that every second counts, and efficiency is the ultimate goal. In contrast, some Eastern cultures approach time in a more fluid, cyclical way, where patience and living in the moment take precedence over the rush to be productive. It's a difference that can shape how people work, how they plan, and even how they live their daily lives.

A Clash of Perceptions About Time

During my time working in India, I encountered something that caught me off guard—a totally different mindset around time. Back home, time is all about deadlines, efficiency, and a sense of urgency. Every moment feels like it's accounted for, and there's always pressure to keep things moving. But in my Mumbai office, it felt like no one was in a rush. Everyone seemed calm, even as deadlines loomed closer. To me, that calmness didn't make sense; it was almost unsettling. How could they be so relaxed with so much to do?

One particular experience sticks out. I had assigned a case study project to my colleagues, outlining every task, setting firm deadlines, and even stressing the importance of reaching out if they ran into any problems. As the deadline approached and I hadn't received any updates or questions, I assumed everything was on track. Then, the day of the deadline arrived, and to my complete shock—almost nothing had been done.

At first, I was frustrated. From where I stood, this looked like a lack of care or urgency, something that would be unacceptable in my work culture. But as I spent more time with the team, I realized this wasn't about laziness or indifference. The problem wasn't their attitude toward the work; it was the fact that they viewed time so differently. They weren't used to the pressure I placed on deadlines, and I wasn't used to their relaxed approach to managing tasks.

What I learned from this was that our misunderstanding wasn't about one culture being right or wrong, but about mismatched expectations. I needed to communicate more clearly and follow-up more frequently about the deadline, while they needed to understand the importance of deadlines in my world. Once we found a way to meet in the middle, everything started to run more smoothly.

Looking back, I wish I had understood the Indian approach to time earlier. If I had, I wouldn't have jumped to conclusions, and my team would have had a better sense of what I expected from them. This experience was a lesson in how important it is to align perspectives when it comes to time, especially when you're working across cultures. It taught me that what looks like 'relaxing' on the outside might just be a different way of dealing with the pressure.

This might be difficult to grasp, and you might even disagree. You may feel like you're constantly stressed at work, rushing from task to task with no time to spare. However, there are still significant differences, and being open to understanding them is the first step. To help you on this journey, consider watching Western business movies such as The Intern, The Pursuit of Happyness, or The Wolf of Wall Street. These films can offer insights and help point you in the right direction.

Flexible Versus Linear Time

During one of my projects in Norway, I worked closely with Anders, the project leader. Having spent ten years in the United States, Anders had a laser-focused mindset on productivity and efficiency. His approach was a constant reminder of the Western way of thinking about time. He would often express frustration: "I've just wasted 30 minutes on this task, and it solved nothing. I could have used that time on something more productive."

This attitude perfectly illustrated the Western work ethic, where every minute is carefully accounted for. Time isn't just a resource—it's a precious commodity that must be maximized. In Western business culture, the phrase "time is money" isn't just a cliché; it's a core principle that drives daily work habits. The origins of this mindset can be traced back to Benjamin Franklin, who famously wrote:

"Remember that time is money. He that can earn ten shillings a day by his labor, and goes abroad, or sits idle for half of that day, though he spends but sixpence during his idleness, ought not to reckon that the only expense; he has really thrown away five shillings besides."

This quote captures the essence of Western attitudes toward time: every moment not spent being productive is seen as a loss, both personally and financially. This philosophy pushes for maximum efficiency, and even short delays or downtime can feel like missed opportunities.

I once spoke with an Indian CEO who shared his experience during a business trip to the U.S. for an important transaction with American executives. The Indian team had traveled to the U.S. for several critical meetings, and after a long morning of intense discussions, they eagerly anticipated lunch as a chance to unwind and build personal connections with their American counterparts.

In Indian business culture, meals aren't just for refueling; they are a key part of business. The Indian CEOs were excited about this opportunity to bond, expecting to share stories, experiences, and enjoy some casual conversation.

However, to their surprise and disappointment, the Americans had scheduled a 30-minute lunch break. For the Americans, this brief lunch was merely a functional pause to grab a quick bite before diving back into work. Their focus on maximizing productivity and efficiency reflected the "time is money" mindset deeply ingrained in Western business practices. There was little room for the leisurely, relationship-focused approach the Indian executives were used to.

The rushed lunch left the Indian visitors disheartened. They had hoped for a more relaxed and extended period to foster deeper connections, something they believed was essential for successful business deals. Instead, the transactional nature of the break felt impersonal, leaving them with the impression that relationship-building was not a priority for their American counterparts.

On the other side of the cultural divide, there's an another story, this time of John, an American executive who traveled to India to negotiate the acquisition of a local consulting company.

From the moment John landed, he was eager to get down to business. He had prepared meticulously for the meetings, bringing detailed presentations and expecting to discuss the finer points of the deal. But to his frustration, the Indian executives approached things differently. For them, using time on relationship-building was a vital part of the process. They wanted to get to know John personally, asking about his family, his interests, and his experiences in India. Instead of getting straight to business, John found himself at elaborate lunches and dinners, where talk of the deal was minimal.

John saw this as inefficient and a waste of time. He felt that valuable hours were slipping away in social pleasantries when there was a deal to finalize. His insistence on sticking to the agenda and focusing on the transaction started to create a disconnect. The Indian executives, sensing his impatience, began to feel that he wasn't interested in fostering a meaningful long-term partnership.

The tension reached a breaking point during one particular lunch. John, glancing at his watch, tried to steer the conversation back to the deal, expressing concern about the timeline. The Indian executives, taken aback by his directness, politely listened but felt that the essential trust and mutual respect had not yet been established.

When John pushed for a quick decision, emphasizing the need to close the deal by the end of the week, the Indian team decided to walk away. For them, the rushed approach undermined the potential for a successful partnership. The focus on immediate gains over relationship-building left them feeling uncertain about the long-term collaboration.

John returned to the U.K. frustrated and disappointed, having failed to secure the acquisition.

The stories highlight how the perception of time varies. These differences often stem from the contrasting views of linear and non-linear time. Erin Meyer has mapped various countries on this timescale and gives the following definitions.

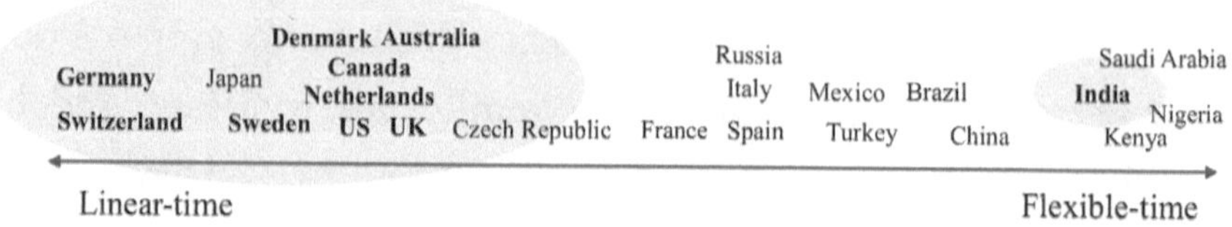

Figure 4.1 Scheduling

Linear time

Project steps are approached in a sequential fashion, completing one task before beginning the next. One thing at a time. No interruptions. The focus is on the deadline and sticking to the schedule. Emphasis is on promptness and good organization over flexibility.

Flexible Time

Project steps are approached in a fluid manner, changing tasks as opportunities arise. Many things are dealt with at once, and interruptions are accepted. The focus is on adaptability, and flexibility is valued over organization.

Source: Eirin Mayer.

This chapter will guide you toward understanding the linear concept of time, present tools on how to adopt, and help you adapt to this working style. Grasping the Western approach to time will shed light on why Westerners often stress over deadlines or seem fixated on their timelines. By learning how time is perceived in the West, you'll be better equipped to align your work habits with their expectations.

When I first started working in India, I didn't understand why my colleagues seemed so relaxed about deadlines – it frustrated me, and I wrongly assumed they didn't care about the work. Over time, I learned that this wasn't the case at all. The difference was cultural, not about motivation or work ethic.

My hope is that by the end of this chapter, you'll fully understand the Western mindset around time. This way, the next time you work with a Westerner, they won't make the same mistaken assumptions about Indians that I once did. I want to ensure that your colleagues and clients see you for who you truly are—dedicated, capable, and efficient—without any misinterpretation clouding that reality.

Evolution of Time Perception

In a Western country like Germany, time is perceived as a structured and rigid resource, deeply influenced by the nation's early industrialization and its cultural emphasis on efficiency. Germans typically view time as finite—something to be managed carefully and used efficiently. This mindset can be traced back to Germany's role as one of the pioneers of industrialization, where punctuality and strict adherence to schedules were essential. For instance, in the German automotive industry, even being a few minutes late could disrupt the entire production process, leading to measurable financial losses. This is a reflection of how deeply ingrained these values are.

This precision-driven view extends into daily life. In Germany, trains are expected to be punctual, traffic systems are highly organized, and regulations are strictly enforced. This predictability allows people to confidently plan their schedules, knowing that external factors won't interfere significantly. In Western cultures like Germany, handling tasks one at a time, in the proper order, is seen as the key to achieving maximum efficiency and productivity.

In contrast, time in India is perceived as more fluid and adaptable, shaped by the country's dynamic and often unpredictable environment. India's socio-economic and historical context has fostered a flexible approach to time, where adaptability and relationship-building often take precedence over strict schedules.

In Indian culture, time is seen as an 'unlimited' resource—something that can be adjusted according to the needs of the moment. This approach isn't just a cultural preference but a necessity in a country where political shifts, financial fluctuations, and natural challenges like monsoons are part of everyday life. Success, particularly in management, is defined by the ability to navigate these changes fluidly, adjusting plans as circumstances evolve.

Navigating Time and Productivity – Perception of coffee breaks

One of the differences I noticed immediately was how breaks are perceived and utilized. In Norway, taking time for a coffee chat or a break often implies that you don't have much to do or that your day isn't as busy as it should be. There's a subtle pressure to remain visibly occupied, and taking frequent breaks could be seen as a sign of idleness or inefficiency.

When I started working in India, however, I was introduced to a completely different approach. My Indian colleagues regularly took breaks for coffee, and even more surprising to me, they encouraged a 'go for a walk' break during the workday. There was even a designated area for walking and refreshing oneself during the day—something I had never seen in my Western experience.

Curious about this practice, I asked my colleagues about it and learned that these breaks were seen as essential to boosting efficiency. They explained how short walks and regular coffee breaks helped clear their minds and rejuvenated their focus when they returned to their tasks. While this concept seemed unfamiliar, I could appreciate the logic behind it and see its potential benefits. Instead of powering through the day without pausing, my Indian colleagues believed that these breaks helped them sustain energy and productivity for longer.

This was quite different from what I was accustomed to in Western culture, where the emphasis is often on continuous work with minimal interruptions. These differences can sometimes lead to misunderstandings in cross-cultural work environments. Western colleagues, particularly those from countries like Norway, might not immediately see the value in frequent breaks and could misinterpret them as a lack of urgency. Conversely, the Indian perspective values the mental rejuvenation that comes from regular pauses. It's not about avoiding work, but about ensuring that when you're working, you're fully present and engaged.

The lesson I took away from this experience is that there isn't a one-size-fits-all approach to productivity. What works in one culture may not resonate in another, but there's value in understanding and adapting to these differences. For Indian professionals working with Western colleagues, it's important to be mindful of how your approach to breaks might be perceived. While you might see regular pauses as a way to enhance your efficiency, your Western counterparts might view it differently. Finding a balance between both perspectives can lead to greater harmony and understanding.

Pursuing Work-Life Balance

In Western cultures, work-life balance is a fundamental principle—a clear separation between professional duties and personal time. This balance emphasizes having a fulfilling life outside of work, whether that involves spending time with friends (who aren't necessarily colleagues), family, or engaging in hobbies and activities unrelated to your job.

Working at one of the big four consultancy firms, a typical workday was packed with non-stop focus from 8 am until 11 am, followed by a quick 30-minute lunch with colleagues. Afterward, I would continue working straight from 12 am until 4 pm, eager to head home and spend time with friends, my girlfriend, or family. Even though I enjoyed my work, the goal was always to carve out enough time for a life outside of it. Work-life balance meant making sure I wasn't consumed by my job. This is an evolving concept in the Western world, where the generation known as baby boomers or Generation X had less work-life balance than the younger generation today, which is Millennials or Generation Z.

To achieve this, we strive for maximum efficiency at work so that we can enjoy our personal time afterward. For example, one particularly productive day for me went like this: I started my morning with a workout from 7 AM to 8 AM, worked efficiently from 8 AM until 4 PM, then spent a couple of hours at a beach from 4 PM to 6 PM. In the evening, I met up with friends to watch the European Championship. This was, in my eyes, a perfect day—a seamless blend of work and life.

Of course, maintaining this balance isn't always possible, especially in high-demand professions like consulting. There were many days working as a consultant where work stretched from early in the morning until long past midnight. During such periods, I found myself eagerly awaiting the weekends to relax and reclaim my personal life.

What truly stood out to me in India was how deeply intertwined social connections were with the workday itself. It wasn't just about taking coffee breaks or casual walks; these moments were integral to building stronger relationships with colleagues. In contrast to the West, where people often separate their personal and professional lives, in India, these bonds are actively nurtured during the workday. Socializing with colleagues isn't seen as something to reserve for after work—it's part of how work gets done.

While forming personal connections with colleagues is certainly valued in Western cultures, in India, it takes on even greater significance. Fostering close, personal relationships at work isn't just encouraged—it's vital to creating a collaborative, harmonious environment. In many ways, work and life blend together seamlessly, and this integration plays a key role in building trust and maintaining a sense of community. Rather than focusing solely on task completion, the Indian approach to work emphasizes relationships, making the workday not only longer but more fulfilling.

Why Time Is so Important

In Western cultures, time is treated with great value, shaping both personal and professional lives. Several key factors drive this deep focus on time:

1. **Efficiency and Productivity:** In Western business environments, time is often viewed as a finite resource that must be managed with precision. The phrase "time is money" reflects the belief that wasted time equals lost opportunities. This perspective fuels a strong emphasis

on punctuality, deadlines, and getting tasks done quickly. It's about maximizing productivity and achieving results without delay.

2. **Work-Life Balance:** Western societies highly value the concept of work-life balance, where there's a clear boundary between work and personal time. The ability to step away from professional duties to enjoy hobbies, spend time with family, or relax is seen as crucial to well-being. Effective time management at work is essential to maintaining this balance, ensuring that work doesn't encroach on personal life.

3. **Punctuality and Reliability:** Punctuality is seen as a sign of respect and professionalism in the West. Arriving late to meetings or social events can be interpreted as disrespectful or unprofessional, undermining trust. Being on time signals reliability and a commitment to honoring others' time.

4. **Structured Schedules:** Westerners typically operate within structured schedules, dividing their day into set blocks for work, meals, and social activities. This predictability allows for careful planning and ensures that commitments are met without unexpected disruptions. A structured approach to time is often linked to success in both personal and professional spheres.

5. **Goal-Oriented Mindset:** In Western cultures, time is tightly linked to achieving specific goals. Whether it's advancing a career, completing a project, or pursuing personal ambitions, time is broken down into tasks and deadlines. This goal-driven approach encourages people to stay focused on priorities and work diligently toward their objectives.

Why is understanding this so important for you? It all comes back to avoiding those frustrating misunderstandings that can easily arise when expectations around punctuality and efficiency aren't met. Many Westerners see time as a reflection of respect. When their time is wasted, they often feel disrespected, which can quickly lead to irritation or even anger.

Imagine this scenario: an Indian professional is in a mid-afternoon check-in video call with their Western manager. They've been working on a project with a tight deadline, and when asked for an update, the Indian colleague casually mentions, "I'm going for a walk." From the Indian's perspective, taking a walk during the workday is a perfectly normal way to clear the mind and regain focus before diving back into the task.

However, the Western manager—already feeling the pressure of the looming deadline—hears this and is taken aback. To them, the idea of taking a walk in the middle of crunch time seems like a distraction or a sign that the task isn't being treated with the urgency it deserves. The manager's immediate thought is, "A walk? We've got this project due soon, and they're stepping away? How are we going to get this done on time?" This builds frustration, with the manager beginning to wonder whether their colleague truly understands the importance of meeting the deadline.

How to Adjust for an Indian

When I was a student, planning my time was key to my success. With exams looming in four weeks, I would meticulously structure a daily plan for all 30 days, breaking down tasks and deciding how many hours to spend on each subject to ensure I was fully prepared. Every hour was accounted for, and each task had its place in the larger goal of acing those exams.

That same approach has followed me into my professional life. I create daily and weekly plans to make sure I'm working as efficiently as possible and meeting the expectations of my managers. And I'm not the only one. Take Jesper, a close colleague of mine—he keeps a running log of tasks and has his workspace covered in post-it notes, each representing a different responsibility or deadline. Why do we do this? Because we understand the stakes. If a partner asks for a task to be done and we forget about it or run out of time, it could leave a lasting negative impression on our development.

It's not always possible to do everything, but the critical part is keeping our managers informed. If we need more time for a task, we say so upfront. Thanks to our running to-do lists, we always have a clear overview of our time and capacity, ensuring nothing slips through the cracks.

This methodical approach—focusing on maximizing every minute—reflects the linear time management mindset, where time is treated as a valuable resource that must be used effectively. Each moment has a purpose, and by structuring our tasks in a linear, step-by-step fashion, we ensure we stay on track and meet our goals.

One approach that has served me well for years is based on the principles from David Allen's book Getting Things Done—a resource I highly recommend. The book introduces a comprehensive system designed to help individuals stay organized and achieve stress-free productivity. Here are the key takeaways:

Capture Everything

Write down every task, idea, or commitment in a trusted system outside your mind. Whether it's a notebook, digital app, or any other tool you use consistently, the goal is to free your brain from the burden of trying to remember every detail.

Clarify Tasks

Once you've captured your tasks, process each one by asking, "What does this mean?" and "What's the next action required?" If a task requires multiple steps, break it down into smaller, actionable items to make it manageable.

Organize Your Tasks

Sort tasks into categories like projects, next actions, or items you're waiting for from others. Use lists and folders to keep related tasks together, making it easy to find what you need to work on next.

Reflect Regularly

Regularly review your lists and systems to keep them updated. A weekly review is highly recommended to ensure you're on track with your goals and adjust your priorities as needed.

Engage with Your Work

When deciding what to work on next, consult your lists. Choose tasks based on context, available time, energy level, and priority. This way, you're always working on the most appropriate task at any given moment.

By following these principles, you will not only achieve a higher level of productivity but also align with the expectations of your Western colleagues. The key is reducing stress by staying organized and ensuring that nothing is forgotten. Allen's method emphasizes the importance of writing down tasks and organizing them effectively, allowing you to focus on what matters most.

Step-by-Step Approach to Time Management:

Building on David Allen's method, here's a practical seven-step approach to help you integrate these time management principles more effectively into your routine:

1. **Prioritize Tasks**

   At the start of each day or week, create a list of tasks in order of priority. This can be done during your commute or first thing in the office. Use planners or apps to help you track tasks and remind yourself of critical deadlines.

2. **Schedule Strictly**

   Allocate specific time slots for each task and include buffer times for any unexpected delays. Stick to these times as closely as possible to ensure you respect the schedule. Treat your time slots with the same commitment you would give to a meeting.

3. **Practice Punctuality**

   Make punctuality a conscious priority for every appointment, deadline, and task. If you foresee a delay, inform your manager or colleagues as soon as possible. View time as a commitment not only to others but also to yourself.

4. **Send Your To-Do List to Your Western Employer or Project Manager**

   Sharing your task list with your manager or team can help align expectations and show your commitment to meeting deadlines. This level of transparency helps build trust and ensures everyone is on the same page.

5. *Embrace Technology*

   Use productivity apps and time management tools to streamline your workflow, set reminders, and improve your efficiency. Apps like Trello, Todoist, or Google Calendar can be particularly useful for managing tasks and ensuring deadlines are met.

6. *Set Boundaries*

   Learn to say no to tasks or invitations that might overcrowd your schedule or detract from your priorities. By setting boundaries, you protect your time and ensure you can focus on what's most important.

7. *Reflect and Adjust*

   At the end of each week, take time to review what you've accomplished and identify areas for improvement. Adjust your strategies based on what worked and what didn't, ensuring continuous progress.

❋ ❋ ❋

Respect time as a limited resource

Time is more than just hours on a clock—it's a reflection of values, culture, and priorities. For Western cultures, time is a finite, structured resource to be maximized. This "time is money" mindset drives efficiency, punctuality, and a goal-oriented focus. For those coming from more flexible time cultures like India, understanding this linear approach is important to navigating and thriving in Western work environments.

By embracing strategies such as prioritizing tasks, scheduling, and practicing punctuality, you can align with Western expectations. This shift not only enhances your work performance but also strengthens trust with your Western colleagues, avoiding critical misunderstandings that can arise from differing time perceptions.

The lessons in this chapter aren't just about being on time – they are about respecting time as a limited resource, as seen through the Western lens. Adapting to this view will improve your efficiency and, more importantly, help you build trust. But earning trust is more complex than just managing time, what else is what the next chapter will cover.

Skill 4: *Embrace the Western view of time as a limited and valuable resource. Focus on efficiency and punctuality to meet expectations and build strong, collaborative relationships.*

Exercise: The Time-Focused Agenda Challenge

Objective: Create a structured daily agenda to maximize productivity and prioritize tasks.

1. **List Key Tasks for the Day:** At the start of your day, write down the top 3-5 tasks that need to be completed. Prioritize them by urgency and impact.

2. **Set Time Blocks:** Assign a specific time block for each task. For example, "10:00-11:00 AM: Finish project proposal" or "2:00-2:30 PM: Client follow-up." Keep blocks realistic, and avoid over-scheduling.

3. **Include Buffer Time:** Plan short breaks or 5-10 minute buffers between tasks to prevent delays from impacting the rest of the schedule.

4. **Stick to the Agenda:** As you move through the day, follow your agenda closely. If an unexpected task arises, adjust by either rescheduling or trimming non-essential tasks.

5

The Currency of Trust: Delivering Results with Consistency

೧✤೧

Building long-term trust through high-quality work and reliability.

Reflection point: Before you begin reading, take a moment to reflect on the three most important elements that make you trust someone at work.

In the West, trust is built brick by brick—each project, each deadline met, lays the foundation for long-term success. But beware, one mistake or misunderstanding can make the whole tower crumble.

Trust is one of the most critical yet elusive elements in any relationship—whether personal or professional. But have you ever wondered how differently trust is built across cultures? In one part of the world, trust might be earned through personal connections and relationships, while in another, it's based on performance and reliability. These differences, while subtle, have a huge impact on how we work and collaborate across borders.

In this chapter, we'll explore the unique ways in which trust is built in India versus Western cultures. Is trust something that develops through close, personal bonds, or is it about proving your competence and reliability? And how do these contrasting approaches affect your ability to succeed in a global workplace?

By the end of this chapter, you'll gain a clearer understanding of how these cultural distinctions influence trust, and you'll be better prepared to navigate the expectations of colleagues from different backgrounds.

Bridging Trust Across Borders

During one of my many conversations about cross-cultural business practices, I came across a particularly insightful story involving a global electronics company headquartered in the United Kingdom. This company, ranked among the top in the world, has operations in fifteen countries, including India and Canada. The story, shared by Priya Nair, the lead negotiator for the Indian team, and her British counterpart, John Wilson, offered a revealing glimpse into the challenges of building trust across cultures.

"The first hour of our meeting in Manchester was filled with introductions," Nair recalled. Dressed in a traditional saree that blended professionalism with cultural pride, she explained how the meeting began with a sense of warmth and camaraderie. "We took some time to get to know each other, sharing brief personal anecdotes. But almost immediately after, the focus shifted to business."

For the next two days, the British and Indian teams worked diligently. The meetings were structured and efficient, with a relentless focus on the tasks at hand. There were brief coffee breaks and quick lunches taken in the conference room. "By 6 pm, the British team would head home, and we would return to our hotel, satisfied with the progress made but also feeling a little disconnected," Nair admitted.

From the British point of view, the pace of the meetings was seen as a sign of respect for the Indian team's time and effort. John Wilson, the British lead, was confident that the direct approach demonstrated professionalism. "We made sure every minute counted," Wilson remarked. "The goal was to be efficient, to maximize our productivity during their visit." "We thought we were being respectful by not wasting time."

But the Indian team, despite appreciating the professionalism, felt something was missing. "We spent two full days together, but I left feeling like we didn't truly know them," Nair said, reflecting on the experience. "They were organized and professional, yes, but without that deeper connection, we weren't fully sure we could rely on their commitments. We didn't feel the trust had been established."

A few weeks later, the British team flew to Mumbai to continue the negotiations. This time, the Indian team wanted to approach things differently. They invited their British counterparts to long lunches and dinners, which often stretched into the late evening. "We wanted to show them our hospitality, to build the personal connection that had been missing in Manchester," Nair explained. "To us, these meals were an important part of establishing trust."

But the British team didn't quite understand. "During that first lunch in Mumbai, I remember checking my watch more than once," Wilson confessed. "I felt a bit uneasy, wondering if we were losing valuable time." "The deadlines were looming, and here we were, spending hours at the table, sharing stories and sampling dishes."

For the British team, trust was built through action—through keeping to schedules, meeting deadlines, and delivering results by understanding the value creation of the deal in terms of return on investment. For the Indian team, trust was rooted in relationships. "These meals weren't just about food," Nair explained. "They were about showing our respect and building a deeper, personal connection." "In India, we believe that if we can trust each other as people, the business will naturally follow."

This clash in approaches led to moments of misunderstanding. The British team, focused on efficiency, struggled to grasp why so much time was being spent on what they saw as peripheral activities. The Indian team, on the other hand, saw these moments as essential. "It wasn't that we weren't taking the negotiations seriously," Nair clarified. "In fact, the opposite was true. By investing time in building trust, we believed we were laying the foundation for a stronger, more reliable partnership."

A Tale of Two Trusts - Relationship versus Task

OptimaTech Pvt. Ltd., a fast-growing tech company in India, had recently expanded its operations into the United States. To break into the Western market, they embarked on a joint venture with Innovatech Inc., a leading software firm based in California.

Ravi Patel, an affable and relationship-focused project manager at OptimaTech, was chosen to lead the Indian team. Ravi firmly believed in the power of building personal connections. He spent hours chatting with colleagues, organizing shared meals, and bonding over coffee breaks. "Trust is built slowly, over time, by truly understanding each other," he often said. This warmth quickly resonated with the Innovatech team, especially with their project lead, Michael Johnson.

"Ravi was a breath of fresh air," Michael recalled. "He made an effort to understand us on a personal level, and it didn't take long before we felt a genuine bond. By the end of the first month, it was as if we had known him for years."

But as the project advanced, cracks began to emerge. The strong personal rapport didn't seem to prevent issues with deadlines and deliverables. Weeks passed, and the quality of work declined. Michael and his team, used to a more task-oriented approach where trust was earned through consistent performance, grew increasingly frustrated.

"The relationship was great, but the project was falling apart," Michael admitted. "We relied on timely, high-quality work, and instead, we were getting delays and apologies."

On the other side, Ravi was puzzled. He believed that the personal relationships he had cultivated would help smooth over any project setbacks. "I've built real friendships here," he thought. "They'll understand that these delays are just temporary."

However, the western team had a different expectation of trust. For them, trust wasn't just about getting along – it was about reliability and consistent results. As deadlines were repeatedly missed, their patience ran out.

The situation reached its peak during a critical client presentation. The Indian team's work was riddled with errors, leaving Michael stunned. "We trusted you, Ravi—not just because we liked you, but because we believed you could deliver," Michael said, his disappointment palpable. "This isn't just about friendship; it's about fulfilling promises."

Ravi was crushed. He had misjudged the balance between relationship-based and task-based trust in this context. Despite the strong personal ties, the project's failure had exposed a critical cultural gap.

What Ravi hadn't fully understood was that in Western business culture, personal rapport can't substitute for professional shortcomings. "We value working with someone we like," Michael explained, "but if the work doesn't meet expectations, it jeopardizes the entire relationship."

Navigating How to Build Trust

As the two stories reflect - In the Western world, trust often begins with a focus on competence and reliability. This is known as **cognitive trust**—the trust you build based on someone's ability to deliver results consistently. When someone meets deadlines, solves problems, and produces high-quality work, cognitive trust grows. It's the professional currency in places like the United States and the U.K., where business relationships are task-oriented. As the stories of John Wilson and Michael Johnson revealed, in Western business culture, trust is often earned not just through personal rapport but through meeting expectations and delivering on promises. This form of trust is practical and task-based. It's about saying, **"I trust you because you do good work."**

On the other hand, **affective trust** is rooted in emotional closeness and personal connection. It's the kind of trust that develops through shared experiences, whether over long meals, casual conversations, or moments of mutual understanding. In cultures like India, affective trust plays a more significant role in business, as relationships are nurtured and strengthened through personal bonds. Priya Nair's story illustrates how, for her team, those long lunches weren't just about food—they were about establishing a deeper connection, building trust by spending time together beyond the confines of strict business discussions. This form of trust is about saying, **"I trust you because I know you and care about you."**

In global business environments, these two forms of trust often overlap, but misunderstandings arise when one side assumes trust will be built through task-based reliability, while the other assumes that personal rapport will carry the day.

Guanxi vs. Networking

In understanding how trust is built across different cultures, it's important to highlight the findings of Roy Chua, a professor at Harvard Business School. His research, titled "Guanxi vs. Networking: Distinctive Configurations of Affect- and Cognition-based Trust in the Networks of Chinese versus American Managers," offers insights into how trust is perceived and developed in American business culture. Chua surveyed executives from a wide range of industries, asking them two fundamental questions: how comfortable they felt sharing personal stories, hopes, and challenges, and how confident they were that their contacts could reliably complete tasks based on their knowledge and competence. His findings underscore the significant role of **cognitive trust** in American professional settings.

In the United States, cognitive trust—the trust built on professional competence, reliability, and performance—is the cornerstone of business relationships. American executives place a strong emphasis on results: meeting deadlines, delivering high-quality work, and solving problems efficiently. While personal rapport can enhance working environments, it never substitutes for cognitive trust. The ability to perform well consistently is non-negotiable, and this task-based trust is what keeps business relationships strong.

Chua's research found that, even though friendship plays a role in trust-building for American executives, it doesn't override the importance of professional reliability. In other words, while personal connections may enhance trust, they are not enough to maintain it in the absence of strong professional competence. Performance and outcomes are what ultimately matter in business interactions.

This contrasts sharply with many Asian cultures, where trust is often a blend of both cognitive and **affective trust**—the trust built on emotional closeness and personal relationships. In cultures like China, the concept of guanxi highlights the importance of personal connections in business. Here, professional competence and personal relationships are intertwined, creating a trust network that's nurtured both through reliable work performance and long-term emotional bonds. Economic exchanges are not just transactional; they serve to strengthen affective trust, which in turn supports business relationships.

In India, trust-building follows a similar path. While Indian professionals understand the importance of delivering quality work, their business relationships are often grounded in personal connections, empathy, and social interactions. Trust develops over shared meals, personal conversations, and informal gatherings. **Affective trust** is cultivated first, creating a strong foundation for professional dealings. But like in the West, **cognitive trust**—the ability to consistently perform well and meet professional expectations—remains crucial. The strength of the relationship depends on both.

Solutions First, Lunch After

A story that highlights how Indians and Westerners think differently about building trust just recently occurred at work for me. We were collaborating with our Indian partner firm, a common practice across Europe. Shakshi, the key lead on their team, was visiting Norway for three days. As soon as my partner heard about this, his immediate reaction was, "What's her objective? What's her plan for these three days?"

No one really knew. "Is she just showing up without a clear agenda?" our managing partner asked, a bit confused. Another director chimed in, "I think she's coming to have a lunch meeting." The partner's response was blunt, "Really? Is she traveling all that way just for lunch? What value does that bring?"

He couldn't understand why Shakshi didn't have a detailed plan or a list of action points to address past issues. We had several problems in the past that needed solutions, and from his perspective, just having lunch was wasting an opportunity. Sitting there, listening, I could sense the gap in understanding. Shakshi wasn't just coming for lunch—she was trying to build trust, the way it's done in many Indian contexts. But my Norwegian colleagues didn't see it that way. To them, her visit seemed unfocused and unproductive.

When I tried to explain that Shakshi was likely aiming to strengthen relationships first, my partners still couldn't connect with her approach. They valued solutions, action plans, and concrete steps to fix the issues at hand. Even though they acknowledged there was a cultural difference, the frustration remained because they wanted solutions on the table, not a meal.

The golden route for Shakshi's visit would have been to balance both approaches. Instead of diving straight into lunch, she could have prepared an agenda and a presentation addressing the specific problems we'd had in the past, showing that she understood the issues and had strategies to fix them. **Solutions first, lunch after.** That would've earned her the trust of my partners, as it would have demonstrated her ability to tackle the tough conversations while still building the personal relationships she was after.

Trusting Scale

Erin Meyer, has dedicated much of her research to understanding cross-cultural management and has developed an insightful tool known as the Trusting Scale. This scale sheds light on the fundamental differences in how cultures around the world build and perceive trust in professional settings. Meyer's Trusting Scale distinguishes between two key forms of trust: **task-based trust,** which is similar to cognitive trust, and **relationship-based trust,** akin to affective trust.

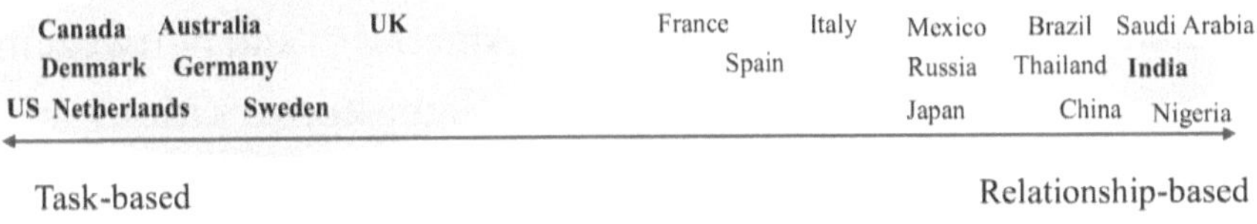

Figure 5.1 Trusting

Task-based trust: Trust is built through business-related activities. Work relationships are built and dropped easily, based on the practicality of the situation. You do good work consistently; you are reliable. I enjoy working with you. I trust you.

Relationship-based: Trust is built through sharing meals, evening drinks, and visits at the coffee machine. Work relationships build up slowly over the long-term. I've seen who you are at a deep level, I've shared personal time with you. I know you well; who trust you, I trust you.

Source: Erin Meyer

Task-based trust is rooted in one's confidence in another's skills, reliability, and professional competence. This form of trust is earned through consistent performance and delivering results. It's a task-oriented approach, most prominent in cultures where professional achievements and capabilities are the cornerstone of business relationships.

On the other hand, relationship-based trust is built on emotional closeness and personal bonds. This type of trust grows from personal interactions, empathy, and shared experiences. It is more relationship-oriented and thrives in cultures where personal connections are crucial to successful business dealings.

Now, you may think this doesn't align with your own experience. Perhaps you've met an American or another Westerner who was friendly and warm in conversation. This is very likely true—Westerners, particularly Americans, are often polite and open in social situations. For instance, Americans and Norwegians may smile at strangers or engage in light conversations with people they barely know. In Norway, for example, it's common to say "hello" to people on the street just out of courtesy.

In the corporate world, you might have encountered American client breakfasts, golf outings, corporate dinners, and parties. These icebreaker activities might seem to suggest that Westerners, like Indians, also build trust primarily through relationships. However, this is not entirely true. These events are typically short and serve a specific purpose: to establish an initial connection.

Once that initial rapport is set, Westerners quickly shift to business. This reflects task-based societies like the United States, the United Kingdom, Australia, and Norway, where relationships are often viewed through a functional and practical lens.

In these cultures, people move in and out of networks easily. If a business relationship isn't working, it's relatively simple to part ways and move on. The focus remains on efficiency, reliability, and results, aligning with the task-based, cognitive trust model, where consistent performance is what truly matters.

As an example, think about how people react when someone on the team is fired. Would you maintain your relationship with that person even though they're no longer part of your company? The answers to this question can vary greatly depending on where you're from. An Indian colleague working in the U.S. once shared this story with me:

"I couldn't believe how my American colleagues responded when one of our team members was let go. One day he was our friend, and the next, it was as if he had disappeared from our lives. I asked my teammates—people I respected— 'When are we going to have a farewell for him? Meet him for drinks? Let him know we're thinking of him?' They looked at me like I was crazy. It seemed like, because he was underperforming, they felt they could just cut him off and act like he didn't matter anymore. As an Indian, this was hard to understand. It was as if they had no emotional bond with either their work or their colleagues.

What I've come to learn is that in India, trust is built on more than just professional performance—it's rooted in deeper emotional bonds. Personal interactions, shared experiences, and genuinely understanding one another are fundamental. Once these connections are made, they aren't easily broken. These bonds endure beyond the workplace, even after someone's professional role has changed or ended.

A personal example of this cultural difference surfaced while I was working on this book. My friend Vatsal, who was reviewing the steps I had outlined, suggested moving 'building relationships' from step ten to step one. For him, relationships are the cornerstone of trust and success, which is a key aspect of Indian business culture.

However, what Vatsal may not fully realize is that in the work environment we shared, his Norwegian colleagues place more importance on his work performance and deliverables. In task-based cultures like mine, professional competence and reliability are the foundation of trust. While friendships and personal relationships certainly matter, they often come after one's ability to perform and contribute professionally.

How to Make the Western Trust You

Earning trust in Western cultures can be seen as a more straightforward process compared to India. In India, trust often hinges on who you know and the depth of your relationships – if you don't have a personal connection, it can be difficult to break into business circles. But in the West, the approach is different. There's a clearer, more transparent path to gaining trust, and it all boils down to one thing: **your performance.**

The formula for trust is simple but powerful:

Deliver high-quality work + meeting expectations + meeting deadlines + being reliable + consistent performance = Trust

---

It's not about who you know but **how well you do your job.** If you can consistently produce excellent work, fulfill commitments, and stay reliable, you'll gain the respect and trust of your colleagues. And this is exactly where you can thrive.

I vividly remember how I learned this the hard way and it is one of the most important lessons I learned early in my career. I had a boss with whom I thought I had built a solid connection—we had shared countless meals, swapped personal stories, and laughed over coffee breaks. I genuinely believed that these moments had cemented our work relationship and made him trust me. But then came a project where I didn't quite deliver the level of quality he expected. I made a few mistakes, nothing too serious, I thought.

I soon found out that the personal rapport we had built didn't matter when the quality of my work slipped. Despite all the meals and conversations, I was bluntly told that the trust in me was gone. That hit me hard. And the way back? It wasn't through more friendly chats or shared dinners. It was through shifting my focus entirely to delivering flawless, reliable work—consistently. Only then did I start to rebuild that trust, piece by piece.

To understand how trust functions differently in India and the West, let's analyze figure 5.2 below. The key insight here is that building a relationship in the West can only take you to what I call "Point C," even if the relationship reaches its peak. Relationship is only a fraction of the *'trust'* equation. *It's important to clarify that this model focuses specifically on trust within work relationships, not personal ones. If we were discussing trust in personal connections, the Indian model would look much more similar to the Western one.*

Now, compare this to 'Point D' in the Indian model. While the level of relationship at 'Point D' is similar to 'Point C' in the Western model, the trust associated with it is significantly higher. This difference highlights a fundamental contrast: in the West, trust in professional relationships operates more independently of personal bonds, whereas in India, trust is closely tied to the depth of the relationship.

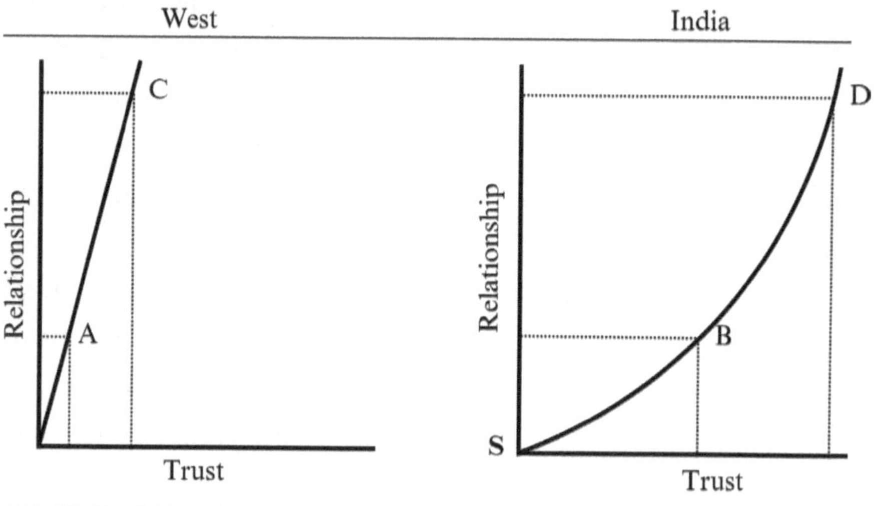

Figure 5.2 Trust versus relationship

As seen in figure 5.2, measuring relationships and trust together doesn't fit the Western model. Figure 5.3 illustrates this by comparing time spent on quality versus building relationships in a Western context. Prioritizing quality over relationships significantly increases trust—shown by the shift from Point C to Point D. While this is a simplified illustration, it underscores a crucial point: the primary objective should always be to deliver high-quality work. If quality falters, trust can decline sharply.

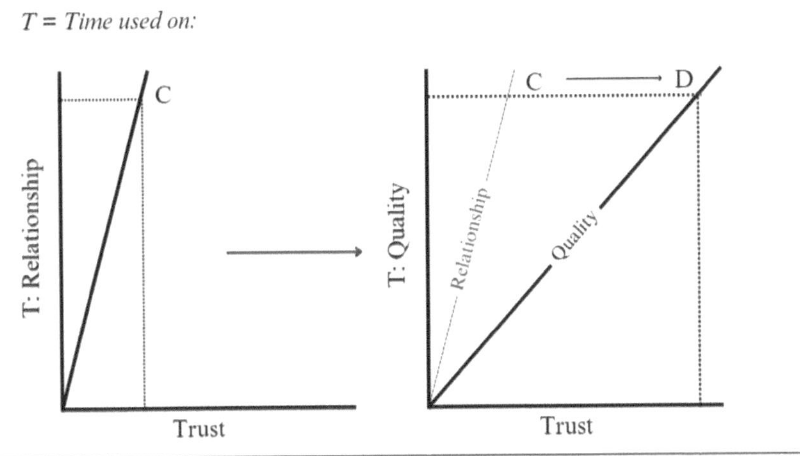

Figure 5.3 Time used on relationship versus quality

Performance-based trust is the cornerstone of Western business culture. In the following sections, I'll describe the key elements of trust outlined in the formula above, encouraging you to embrace these principles. I know the significant impact they will have on your success.

What Does 'High-Quality Work' Really Mean?

Delivering high-quality work is the foundation of building trust in any Western workplace. It's not just about completing tasks; it's about executing them with a level of excellence that demonstrates your reliability and competence. When you deliver consistent, high-quality work, you naturally inspire confidence in your abilities. So, what does it take to ensure your work consistently meets Western standards? Here's a breakdown of key elements that will help you achieve that:

Understand the Task Completely: Before you can deliver, you need to fully grasp what's expected of you. If something isn't clear, ask. Clarifying any uncertainties early on shows that you're serious about doing the job right. Western colleagues appreciate this because it shows you're committed to delivering exactly what's needed and that you're not afraid to ensure you're on the right track.

Reflection point: Going forward you should: Before starting, summarize the task requirements back to your manager or client in your own words. This helps confirm that you've understood the task fully and allows them to clarify any details upfront.

Avoid Sloppy Mistakes: Attention to detail is everything. One small error can send the message that you didn't care enough to double-check your work. Make sure your work is free of grammatical errors, formatting mistakes, or miscalculations. Use proofreading tools, review style guidelines, and take the time to ensure your final product is polished. Remember, every detail counts.

Reflection point: Going forward you should: Build in time at the end of each task to proofread and double-check for errors, even small ones. Use a checklist to review grammar, formatting, calculations, or any other key details specific to the project.

Aim to Impress: Completing the task is important, but exceeding expectations is where you can really make an impact. Spend an extra 30-60 minutes thinking of how you can elevate the work. Could you provide additional insights or suggest improvements that weren't part of the original request? By taking the initiative and offering something beyond what was asked, you show a commitment to excellence. This is a powerful way to demonstrate your value and build trust.

Going forward you should: Once the task is done, spend an extra 30-60 minutes considering how you can add value. This might mean providing a quick summary of insights, adding an improvement suggestion, or highlighting a useful trend you noticed during your work.

Meeting Expectations

Meeting expectations is one of the most critical aspects of maintaining and deepening trust in any professional environment. When we talk about meeting expectations, we mean consistently delivering on the standards and requirements set by your colleagues, managers, and the organization. Here's why it's so important, and how you can master it:

Establishing Professional Credibility: Consistently meeting expectations is the cornerstone of building professional credibility. It shows that you not only understand what's required but that you can reliably deliver. Over time, this builds a strong foundation of trust, as your colleagues and managers come to see you as someone who can **be counted** on to meet or **exceed** the standards set for you. Each time you **meet expectations**, you reinforce this trust.

Enhancing Your Reputation: Colleagues and managers remember who they can depend on, and those individuals are often rewarded with more opportunities, increased responsibilities, and even career advancement.

Engaging with Feedback: A key part of meeting expectations is actively engaging with feedback—both giving and receiving it. Regular feedback ensures that you're aligned with what's expected and provides a valuable opportunity to adjust your approach as needed. By continuously improving based on feedback, you not only meet but often exceed expectations, deepening trust in the process.

Addressing Misunderstandings Early: Sometimes expectations aren't communicated clearly, or they may change mid-project. When this happens, it's vital to address any misunderstandings or misalignments as quickly as possible. Clarifying ambiguous expectations or confirming changes early prevents bigger issues down the line, helping to maintain your credibility and ensuring you stay on track.

Balancing High Expectations and Risk: High expectations can be a powerful motivator, driving you to push boundaries and achieve more. But they also come **with risks.** If you set expectations too high and **fail** to meet them, it can lead to disappointment and **erode** the trust you've worked so hard to build. Balancing ambition with realism is key—setting goals that are both challenging and attainable will keep you growing while ensuring you maintain the trust of those around you.

Unfortunately, throughout my experience working with colleagues in India, I often found that the high expectations they set for themselves weren't met. There were times when I received inaccurate information or felt that my colleagues assured me they had everything under control, only to discover later that they didn't. I also encountered situations where managers presented consultants as highly experienced, only to realize they required much more guidance than initially suggested.

It took me some time to understand that these issues stemmed largely from communication misunderstandings. There were likely subtle cues and indirect ways of conveying information that I missed, as I was used to a more direct style of communication, with reference back to the chapter on communication. In cross-cultural settings, particularly when working with Western colleagues, being 100% direct and truthful about your capabilities and the expectations you're setting is absolutely crucial. Remember, they tend to take your words at face value and trust that you mean exactly what you say.

Setting expectations that you're unable to meet immediately breaks trust, and it can take significant time and effort to rebuild. Clear, honest communication is essential, especially when dealing with colleagues from cultures that place a high value on reliability and straightforwardness. By being transparent about what you can deliver, you ensure that everyone is on the same page, avoiding the disappointment and frustration that come from misaligned expectations.

A close friend of mine, a lawyer named Joachim, taught me a powerful lesson: always "under promise and overdeliver." Instead of setting sky-high expectations, they set them slightly lower, with the sole purpose of exceeding them. This approach creates significant value and builds trust, avoiding the risk of overpromising and underdelivering—a mistake that can quickly drive clients away.

The figure below illustrates this concept. In Scenario 1, you "under promise" by committing to complete 6 tasks. Although your best-case scenario is 10 tasks, you know that realistically you can complete 8. When you end up delivering 9, you've exceeded the client's expectation of 6, leaving them pleasantly surprised and highly satisfied.

In Scenario 2, you promise to complete 10 tasks, aiming high but aware it's a stretch. You still end up completing 9 tasks, but this time, the client feels disappointed because they expected 10. Despite delivering the same amount of work, the client's perception shifts from satisfaction to disappointment due to the unmet promise.

This example shows the power of managing expectations. By under promising and overdelivering, you can consistently exceed client expectations, building trust and long-term satisfaction.

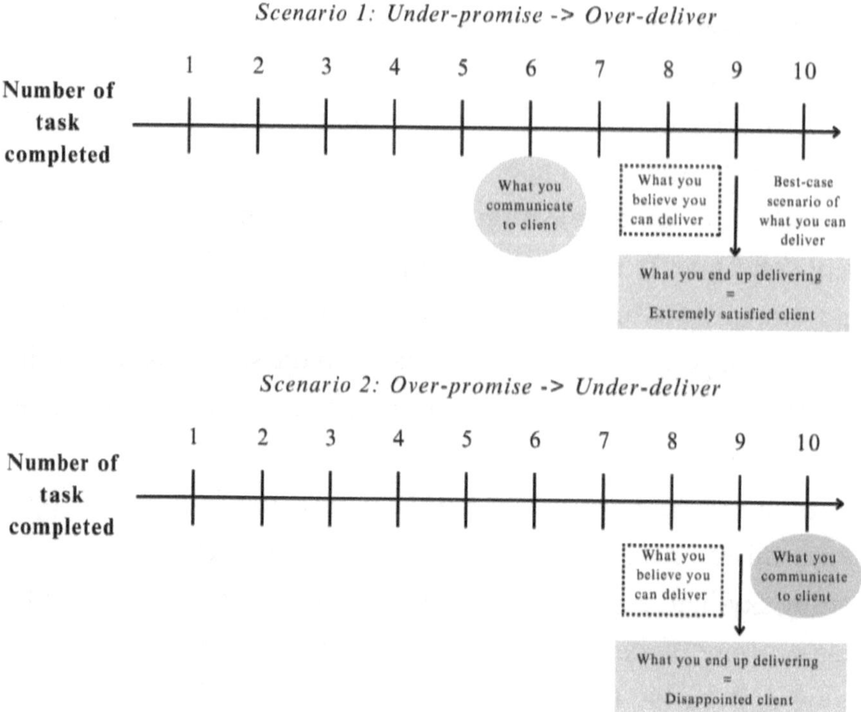

Figure 5.2 Over and under-promise on delivery

As you continue reading, remember the importance of always communicating your expectations openly and ensuring you fully understand the expectations others have of you. This simple practice will help you build a solid foundation of trust and lead to smoother, more productive collaborations.

- **Clarify Expectations Early:** Ask direct questions like, "What's the most important outcome for this project?" to ensure alignment from the start.
- **Confirm Deadlines:** Don't assume—ask, "Is there a specific deadline or milestone you have in mind?"
- **Assess Your Capacity:** Evaluate your workload honestly, and communicate realistic timelines. If needed, say, "To ensure quality, I'll need until [date]. Does that work?"
- **Set Regular Check-Ins:** Suggest brief updates, like, "Would a weekly update help keep us aligned?"

- **Under promise, Overdeliver:** Set achievable goals, and aim to exceed them. This approach leaves clients pleasantly surprised and builds lasting trust.

Deadlines

Deadlines are a critical component of professional environments, serving as benchmarks for progress and ensuring that projects stay on track. Meeting deadlines is not just about time management; it's also deeply connected to trust. As discussed in the chapter on time, deadlines are viewed as firm commitments in Western cultures—missing them can lead to a breakdown in trust and credibility. Addressing missed deadlines immediately, understanding the reasons behind them, and working with the team to find solutions is crucial to preventing future occurrences. Here's why deadlines hold such importance for Western colleagues and what you should consider to ensure they are met:

Maintaining Professionalism: Meeting deadlines is a key indicator of professionalism. It shows that you take your responsibilities seriously and respect the time and effort of others involved in the project. In Western cultures, consistently missing deadlines doesn't just impact a project—it impacts your reputation.

Ensuring Project Progress: Deadlines keep projects moving forward and ensure that momentum is maintained. In complex projects, each missed deadline creates delays that ripple through the entire timeline. Western colleagues often view these delays as inefficiencies, eroding trust in both the individual and the team's ability to deliver results.

Facilitating Planning and Coordination: Deadlines enable effective planning and coordination within teams. When deadlines are met, team members can better align their efforts, resources, and schedules. Consistency in meeting deadlines minimizes bottlenecks, improving workflow efficiency. This is crucial in task-based trust cultures, where smooth coordination and timely execution are highly valued.

The figure below illustrates this concept of under and over-promise in terms of deadlines. In **Scenario 1**, you "under promise" by committing to deliver in 8 days. Although your best-case scenario is 3 days, you know that realistically you can deliver in 6. When you end up delivering in 5 days, you've exceeded the client's expectation of 8, leaving them pleasantly surprised and highly satisfied.

In **Scenario 2**, you promise to deliver in 3 days, aiming high but aware it's a challenge. You still deliver in 5 days, but this time, the client feels disappointed because they expected it sooner. Despite delivering in the same number of days, the client's perception shifts from satisfaction to disappointment due to the unmet promise.

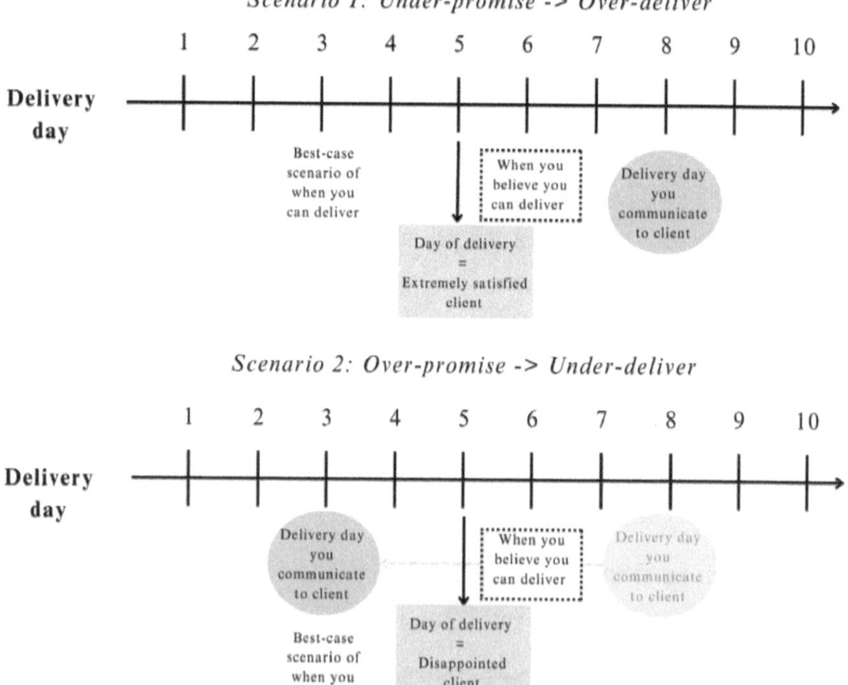

Figure 5.3 Over and under-promise on delivery day

Reliability

Reliability is one of the most fundamental aspects of building trust in Western work environments. When colleagues and managers consider you reliable, they believe in your ability to consistently meet commitments, deliver on promises, and maintain a steady, dependable presence. This confidence in your reliability forms the bedrock of professional relationships and long-term success. Let's dive into what being reliable truly means and how you can embody this crucial trait:

Delivering on Promises: When you make a commitment, whether it's a minor task or a significant project, **following through** is essential. Delivering on promises strengthens trust and shows that you are someone who can be counted on. In task-based cultures like those in the West, reliability isn't just about doing the job—**it's about doing it when you said you would.**

Proactive Communication: Keeping your team and managers informed about your progress, potential roadblocks, or changes that might affect your ability to deliver on time helps manage expectations. This proactive approach prevents last-minute surprises and shows that you take your commitments seriously. It's not just about meeting the deadline – it's about ensuring everyone is aware of where things stand along the way.

Dependable Presence: Your presence—both physical and virtual—matters. Being available when needed, attending meetings on time, and being reachable for important communications all contribute to your reliability.

To build trust through reliability, here are some key questions you can ask your Western clients to align expectations and demonstrate commitment:

1. **Delivering on Promises**

   - "To make sure we're on the same page, what aspects of this project are most critical for you?"
   - "Are there specific deadlines or milestones you consider essential? This will help me plan my timeline effectively."

2. **Proactive Communication**

   - "How often would you like updates on our progress? I want to make sure I'm keeping you informed in a way that works for you."
   - "If any issues or delays come up, how would you prefer I communicate them? Would you like immediate updates or a plan with possible solutions?"

3. **Flexibility and Adaptability**

   - "Are there any changes to the project's scope or timeline I should anticipate? This will help me stay prepared and adaptable."
   - "If priorities shift, how would you like me to handle that? I want to make sure I can adjust effectively while meeting your expectations."

4. **Dependable Presence**

   - "Are there key times or meetings where my presence is especially important to you? I want to ensure I'm available when needed."
   - "What's your preferred way to reach me if something urgent comes up? That way, I can respond quickly when it matters most."

These questions show your commitment to delivering on promises, communicating proactively, and adapting when necessary—all of which build a strong foundation of trust and reliability in Western work environments.

Consistency

Consistency is the foundation upon which all the bricks of trust are built. It is the final, most crucial, and often the hardest component that holds everything together. Without consistency, even the most well-intentioned efforts to establish trust can quickly crumble. Here's why consistency is vital and how it shapes professional relationships:

Building a Reputation of Dependability: Consistency is the cornerstone of reliability. Performing at a high level on an occasional basis is not enough; you need to deliver results consistently. Colleagues and managers should know they can count on you to meet expectations every time, not just when conditions are favorable. A steady track record of high-quality work builds your reputation as dependable and competent.

The Fragility of Trust: Trust, once built, is fragile. It's developed over time, through repeated actions that reinforce reliability. However, trust can be broken much faster than it took to create. You can deliver excellent work ten times in a row, but if you fail once, it can significantly damage the trust you've built.

The Impact of Inconsistency

Inconsistency creates doubt. If your performance fluctuates, colleagues and managers may start to question whether they can rely on you. Inconsistent behavior will hinder collaboration and lead to an environment of uncertainty. If people are unsure whether you will meet your commitments, trust—and the entire working relationship—becomes unstable.

Strategies for Maintaining Consistency

Set Realistic Goals: Ensure that your commitments are achievable within the time and resources available. Overpromizing can lead to failure, so manage expectations wisely.

Stay Organized: Use tools and systems to keep track of tasks, deadlines, and priorities. Organization is key to maintaining consistent performance.

Prioritize Quality: Even when faced with challenges, strive to deliver high-quality work. Maintaining high standards is critical to being consistent.

Seek Feedback: Regular feedback helps you stay on track and ensure you're meeting expectations. It also offers insights into areas for improvement.

Building Trust Across Continents

In the bustling city of Bengaluru, Rajiv Menon sat at his desk, eyes glued to his computer screen, meticulously reviewing the final touches on a report for an Australian client. He was a remote project manager working with a prominent software firm in Melbourne, Australia, and, though he had never met his team face-to-face, Rajiv was determined to earn their trust through hard work and consistency.

Rajiv's journey with the Australian firm started with a small pilot project. "It's a test," he told himself. "If I can prove my worth here, more opportunities will come." He knew that his Western clients valued punctuality, high standards, and a professional approach. Rajiv had a plan to impress them by meeting expectations, delivering high-quality work, and respecting deadlines.

On his first day, Rajiv had a virtual call with his manager, Emma. She was an experienced project lead and set clear expectations from the start.

"Rajiv, welcome to the team! I know you're working remotely, and I want to make sure you're comfortable with the workload," Emma started, a touch of reservation in her tone.

"Thank you, Emma. I'm ready for the challenge. I believe in open communication, so please let me know if there's ever an area where I can improve or add more value," Rajiv replied confidently.

Emma gave him a brief overview of the project timeline and deliverables. "The client expects a comprehensive analysis and a detailed action plan by the end of this month. It's a tight deadline, but we need to ensure there's no compromise on quality," she said.

"Absolutely, Emma. I'll send updates every week and make sure we're on track," Rajiv assured her.

In the coming days, Rajiv put in long hours to familiarize himself with the client's expectations and deliver exceptional quality. Despite the time difference, he scheduled overlapping hours so he could connect directly with his Australian teammates and managers. He aimed to stay consistent, reliable, and proactive, knowing these qualities were key to establishing trust with a Western team.

One morning, Rajiv received a message from Emma. "Rajiv, we're a bit concerned about a delay on the reporting software integration. Do you have an update on that?"

Rajiv immediately replied, "I've anticipated that delay, Emma. To stay on schedule, I prepared an alternative solution, and I can walk you through it now if that helps."

Emma was impressed. "You're really on top of things, Rajiv! I appreciate your proactive approach," she said with a sense of growing trust.

As weeks turned into months, Rajiv's performance remained consistent. He never missed a deadline, consistently exceeded quality benchmarks, and was always one step ahead with solutions for potential roadblocks. His colleagues, who were initially hesitant, soon began to rely on him. One day, during a team meeting, his colleague from Australia, Ben, admitted, "Rajiv, I wasn't sure how the remote arrangement would work, but honestly, I feel like you're just as invested as any of us here in Melbourne. It's really great working with you."

Emma echoed the sentiment in their next one-on-one. "Rajiv, you've earned our trust. Your consistency and dedication have made you an invaluable part of the team. I'll be recommending you for a lead role on the next big project," she said with a proud smile.

Prove yourself through consistent action

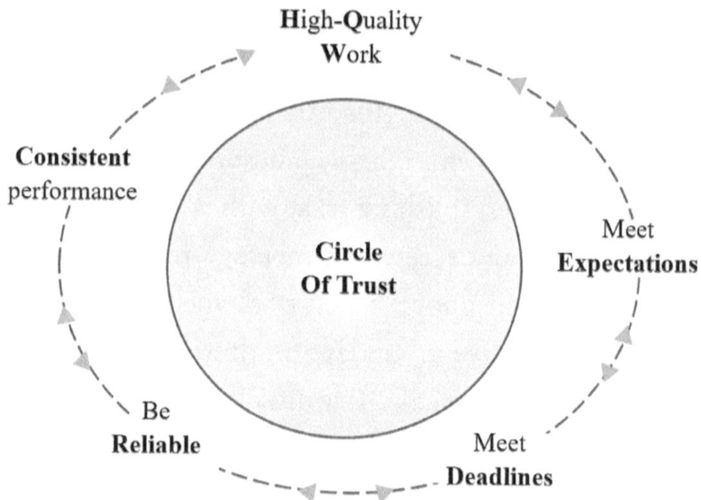

Figure 5.3 Circle of trust

In wrapping up this chapter, it's clear that trust in Western work environments goes beyond personal connections. It's about proving yourself through consistent action, delivering on your commitments, and being someone your colleagues and clients can depend on. In these cultures, trust is built slowly, not through meals but one reliable action at a time, and it's sustained by showing that you can perform at a high level time and again.

As you move forward in your career, keep these principles in mind. Approach every task with care, ensure that you meet expectations with precision, and when something doesn't go as planned, be upfront about it. This is how you build a reputation that others can trust.

Think of trust as a bridge. Every successful project, every met deadline, and every honest conversation is a brick in that bridge. Over time, as you keep laying those bricks, the trust you've built will stand strong. It's a continuous process, one that's crucial for long-term success in western work environments. But be aware, the truth is that you can deliver ten good projects, but one bad will make the whole structure crumble, and you need ten more to regain your trust - and it's not guaranteed that you will get that opportunity.

To wrap up, here's the best advice: as you begin working with a client or colleague, invest time in truly understanding what they expect from you. Start by researching their past projects to get a sense of their style and goals. Then, ask open questions and clarify what success looks like to them. Meeting these expectations is one of the most reliable ways to build trust.

In the next chapter, we'll dive into the art of convincing and selling. With the foundation of trust firmly in place, you'll learn how to use it to influence, persuade, and build compelling arguments that resonate with your Western counterparts. The ability sell your ideas and convince others will rely heavily on the trust you've established—let's build on that.

Skill 5: *Build trust by **consistently** delivering **high-quality** work and **reliably** meeting **expectations** and **deadlines**.*

Exercise: Expectation Alignment Checklist

For your next project, try this simple exercise to ensure you and your Western counterpart are fully aligned on expectations. Clear communication at the start can make a large difference in building trust and delivering exactly what's needed.

Objective: Quickly align with Western counterparts by clarifying and confirming expectations.

1. **Ask for Specifics:** At the start, ask, "What does a successful outcome look like?" and "Are there specific details you want included?" Write down their answers.

2. **Define Milestones Together:** Propose key checkpoints (e.g., "Let's review the first section by [date]") to confirm progress meets expectations. Should be within days after start.

3. **Create a Pre-Delivery Checklist:** Before final submission, check each requirement to ensure you've met every expectation discussed.

4. **Request Feedback:** After delivery, ask, "Did this meet your expectations?" Use any feedback to adjust for future tasks.

6

Pitch Perfect: Convincing with Clarity and Confidence

 summary

Mastering the art of delivering concise, solution-driven arguments to persuade anyone in the West

You've come a long way. By now, you've sharpened your skills in communication, learned the art of starting new relationships, handling time and mastered how to establish trust with Western colleagues. These are fundamental building blocks. But now comes the next challenge—the skill that separates the good from the great: the ability to convince and sell.

Before you think, 'I'm not in sales, this doesn't apply to me', consider this: we're all selling something, all the time. You may not be selling a product, but you're always selling your ideas, your work, and most importantly, yourself. Whether you're pitching a project to a client, negotiating a raise with your boss, or simply making a case for your approach in a team meeting—convincing others is a skill you'll need throughout your career.

Let me paint a few scenarios. Imagine you're wrapping up a cross-border IT project and preparing your final presentation for a U.K. client. You've done the hard work, and now you need to showcase the results in a way that not only satisfies but convinces the client of the immense value you've delivered. Or maybe you've just moved to the U.S., eager to prove yourself in your first marketing role. You have the ideas, but how do you present them in a way that resonates with your American boss?

It doesn't stop there. Think about a job interview, where your ability to 'sell' your skills and experience is the difference between landing your dream job or getting passed over. Or maybe you've been working for the same company for years and now feel it's time for a promotion or a raise. How do you make your case in a way that convinces your manager you deserve it?

The truth is, knowing how to convince and sell is not just about closing deals or working in sales. It's about being able to influence and persuade in any professional setting. It's the difference between having great ideas and getting people to buy into them. It's what turns good work into recognized, appreciated, and rewarded work.

This chapter is about mastering that next skill: how to take what you've learned about communication, trust, and relationships and elevate it. How to be clear, concise, and compelling. How to present solutions in a way that makes people say, "Yes, that's exactly what we need."

At its core, selling is universal. Zig Ziglar, one of the most renowned sales experts, once said:

"Selling is essentially a transfer of feelings."

—Zig Ziglar

This rings true no matter where you are—in the West or India. But here's the catch: the way that transfer happens, how those feelings are communicated and received, varies greatly between cultures. And that's precisely what this chapter will address.

Take Steve Jobs as an example. He once famously said,

"People don't know what they want until you show it to them."

—Steve Jobs

Jobs' brilliance wasn't just in creating innovative products but in his unmatched ability to convince others of his vision. His persuasive presentations didn't just sell products— they sold ideas, dreams, and a future. He got his team and customers to see the world through his eyes. This principle applies in India and the West, but the difference lies in how you 'show' them.

Albert Einstein once said,

"If you can't explain it simply, you don't understand it well enough."

—Albert Einstein

The key to convincing others, especially in the West, is how you explain your ideas. Simplicity and clarity are non-negotiable. It's not just about having the best solution—it's about making sure that the solution is understood, absorbed, and trusted by the people you're trying to convince.

This is why understanding your audience is so critical. Before you can hope to persuade anyone, you need to sit down, listen, and fully grasp the issues they care about. This principle is one of the cornerstones of Stephen Covey's best-selling book, *The 7 Habits of Highly Effective People*. In it, he writes, "Seek first to understand, then to be understood." Covey's point is simple: to sell effectively, you must first ensure you truly understand who you are selling to and what their needs are.

So, in this chapter, we're going to explore exactly how to 'show' people what they need, how to transfer your feelings to them in a way that resonates, and how to convince them that your solution is the right one—every time.

The Misjudged Pitch

Vikram Patel, an experienced IT consultant from Mumbai, was gearing up for what he believed could be the most important presentation of his career. He was set to pitch his company's latest software solution to a prominent firm in New York. Back home in India, Vikram had always found success through personal connections before diving into the technical aspects of a deal. His clients valued these moments, and it had never failed to open doors.

With this in mind, Vikram began his presentation in New York the same way—by sharing stories about his experiences, the journey of his company, and the relationships they had built with their clients. In Mumbai, this approach had always warmed up the room, creating a sense of camaraderie before the business discussions began.

But as Vikram spoke, something felt different. The executives listened quietly, their expressions unreadable. They nodded politely but offered little else. Confident that this was just their style, Vikram continued, believing the connection would come with time. After all, in India, these personal stories laid the groundwork for trust and partnership.

As the minutes ticked by, the atmosphere didn't shift. Some of the executives exchanged glances, and Vikram noticed subtle signs of restlessness—quick glances at watches, the occasional shuffle in a seat. He started to feel a growing unease but kept going, convinced that he was setting the right tone.

Then, midway through his presentation, Sarah, the lead executive, politely cut in. "Mr. Patel, your stories are interesting, but could we dive into the technical details? We're eager to understand how your software will integrate with our systems."

Vikram hesitated. This was much earlier in the conversation than he had expected. He had planned to build up to the technical specifics after laying a personal foundation, but clearly, the room was looking for something else. Quickly adjusting his slides, he launched into the technical overview, but the flow of the presentation had shifted, and he could feel the difference.

The executives, however, started engaging more as soon as he discussed the software's functionality. They asked pointed questions about data security and scalability, focusing on the specifics of what his product could do. The earlier warmth he'd tried to create hadn't landed the way he expected, and now, with time running out, he was left trying to recover.

When the meeting ended, Sarah offered a polite "We'll follow-up," but Vikram could sense that something had been lost. On his flight back to Mumbai, he replayed the presentation in his mind. He had delivered his usual approach—personal, relational, thoughtful—but it hadn't resonated. Instead of the connection he had hoped to build, he had found himself scrambling to meet the client's expectations.

As he thought about it more, Vikram was left with questions: Why had his approach fallen flat here? What had he missed? Why were the American executives so eager to jump straight into the technical details?

Vikram's experience highlights a common challenge many face when navigating Western business environments: understanding how to balance personal rapport with professional efficiency.

How to Sell

The fundamentals of convincing and selling in India and Western countries seem similar. The process begins with understanding your client's needs—how can you persuade or sell something if you don't know what they need? After that, you present your solution, or in other words, make your pitch. These steps are universal. But despite the commonality in approach, there are fundamental differences in how these steps play out across cultures. So, how are they the same yet different?

In both cultures, the foundation of a successful sale or convincing argument is trust. If you don't trust the person trying to sell or persuade you, no deal is going to happen; you're out— *"Nahi banega, Koi sauda nahin."* But as we discussed in the previous chapter, trust is built differently in India compared to the West, and this plays a crucial role in the selling process as well. It's important to remember the distinction between business-related trust (with colleagues and clients) and personal trust (with friends and family).

In India, trust is often established early in the process, even before the selling or convincing begins. It's common to try to form a personal relationship with the person you're trying to persuade before diving into the business discussion. Once this relationship is built, the trust is there, and the seller can then move forward with understanding the client's needs and offering a solution.

In contrast, Western cultures approach this in the opposite direction. Trust isn't established through relationship-building at the outset; instead, it comes after the pitch. From the perspective of a Western client, trust is built if the salesperson or adviser demonstrates a clear understanding of the client's problem and offers a solution that directly addresses it. Therefore, in the West, it's completely normal—to sell to someone you've just met, without any prior relationship. This is why it's entirely possible to sell to a stranger, build trust through your expertise, and move forward.

At the core of convincing and selling is the simple truth: you need to know your client's problem, and you need to offer a solution that addresses it. This is where trust begins to form— not as a separate stage but throughout the entire process. As you ask the right questions and genuinely listen, you begin building a relationship, even as you work to present your solution. In this sense, selling and forming a relationship **happen simultaneously,** rather than as **distinct steps.** The relationship is built as you understand their needs and as you demonstrate your expertise in solving their problems. These are the two pillars this chapter will explore.

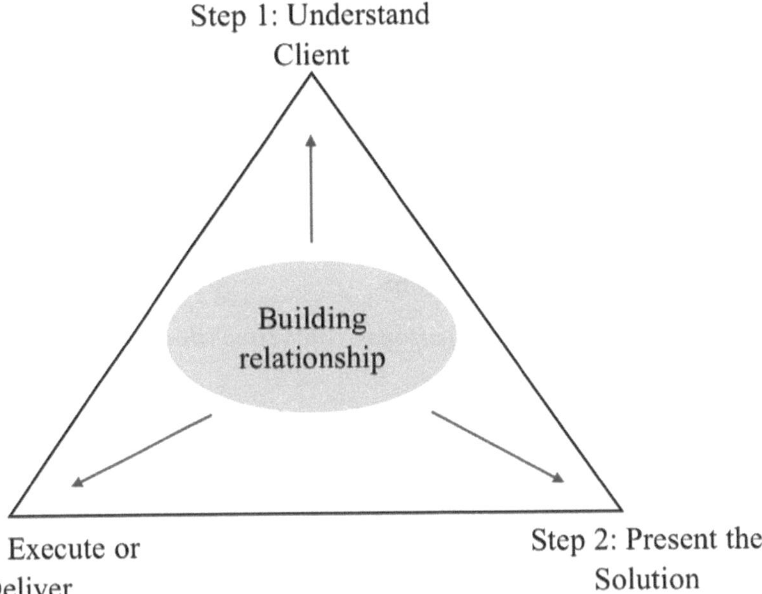

Figure 6.1 Western Trust Model

Step 1: Understand the Client's Needs

Focus: Listening to and identifying the client's problems.

Outcome: Trust begins to form as the client feels understood.

Step 2: Present the Solution

Focus: Offering a well-thought-out, solution-focused approach to the problem.

Outcome: Trust is strengthened when the solution addresses the client's needs effectively.

Step 3: Execute or Deliver

Focus: Consistently following through with high-quality work.

Outcome: Trust is solidified by consistent performance.

Relationship-Building *overlays the entire process. Rather than a separate step,* **building relationships** *is integrated into each of the three steps. The relationship develops as you show your competence in understanding, presenting, and delivering solutions. You don't need to build a relationship beforehand; the* *relationship evolves naturally as trust is earned through competence and reliability.*

Step 1: Establish Relationship	Step 2: Understand Client Needs	Step 3: Present and Deliver

Figure 6.2 Indian Trust Model

Step 1: *Establish Relationship*

Focus: Forming a personal connection through trust and mutual understanding.

Outcome: Without this step, it's difficult to proceed with the business transaction.

Step 2: *Understand the Client's Needs*

Focus: After establishing the relationship, you then proceed to listen and identify the client's needs.

Outcome: Trust deepens as you show care for the client's problems.

Step 3: *Present and Deliver the Solution*

Focus: Offering a solution that addresses the client's issues.

Outcome: Trust is now solidified through both the relationship and your ability to deliver the solution.

*Here, **building relationships** is step 1, the foundation upon which the rest of the process depends. Without first establishing trust through relationship-building, it's difficult to move forward to understanding the client's needs or presenting a solution.*

Elevator Pitch

Before we dive into practical techniques on how to sell and convince effectively, there's a key concept you need to remember from the chapter about time: Westerners highly value efficiency, time is money. In a Western setting, time is precious, and if you want to convince someone, you have to do it fast. That's why the idea of an 'elevator pitch' exists – if you can't communicate the essence of your idea in under a minute, you've probably already lost their attention.

> *An elevator pitch is a brief (think 30-60 seconds!) way of introducing yourself, getting across a key point or two, and making a connection with someone. It's called an elevator pitch because it takes roughly the amount of time you'd spend riding an elevator with someone.*

This means that in the West, while relationships are important, they often take a back seat during the early stages of a sales or persuasion process. What truly matters in those first moments is how clearly and efficiently you can communicate your proposal. Western clients expect you to focus on the problem they are facing, present a solution efficiently, and give them the confidence that you can deliver—all without wasting their time.

Understand Your Client, College, and Customer Needs

Neil Rackham, a British author and consultant, wrote the book *"SPIN Selling"* – introducing a new way of thinking about how we sell, shifting the focus toward understanding the customer's problems and offering tailored solutions. Rackham's research is a reminder that successful selling is not about pushing a product or idea, but about solving a problem the client may not even realize they have.

Rackham's SPIN framework—Situation, Problem, Implication, and Need-Payoff—provides a roadmap for uncovering those deeper needs. It helps you navigate beyond surface-level issues and delve into the challenges that are holding your client back. By mastering this approach, you're not just selling a product; you're creating meaningful dialogue, fostering trust, and building long-term relationships.

Even if you don't have a chance to speak directly with your client before presenting your value proposition, you can still apply the SPIN technique. Do your research. Anticipate what your client's needs might be and frame your pitch around those assumptions. The beauty of this method is that it's adaptable, giving you a structure to work with even when you're working off limited information.

Now, let's delve deeper into the SPIN framework. This will guide you in building a compelling and tailored value proposition that resonates with your Western clients.

SPIN Selling

SPIN Selling[1] revolves around four key types of questions: Situation, Problem, Implication, and Need-Payoff. These structured questions form the backbone of uncovering your client's true needs and crafting a solution that resonates. One of the most effective ways to convince a Westerner is to quickly tell them what they want to hear, but the challenge lies in knowing exactly what they want. This is where the SPIN technique comes in—it helps you get straight to the heart of their needs. Here's how to use it:

1. *Situation Questions: Setting the Scene*
   Purpose: To gather crucial background information about the client's current state. These questions help you understand the context in which the client operates.

---

1   *For more practical examples on how to apply SPIN-selling techniques to communicate effectively with Western clients, visit www.larshelgesen.com.*

Examples:

"Can you describe your current process for managing projects?"

"What systems are you using for inventory management?"

Tips:

Keep these questions brief to avoid overwhelming the client.

Do your homework. Research their industry, company, recent news, and competitors to ask sharp, relevant questions.

Example:

You're meeting an e-commerce client and discover they've recently expanded to international shipping. You can ask: "I noticed you've started shipping internationally. What logistics platform are you using for these operations?"

2. *Problem Questions: Identifying Pain Points*

   Purpose: To uncover specific issues or frustrations the client is facing, identifying where your solution can help.

   Examples:

   "What challenges are you facing with your current system?"

   "Are there aspects of your process that you find particularly frustrating?"

   Tips:

   Listen actively and empathize with their struggles. This helps build rapport and trust.

   Research common industry challenges so you can anticipate their issues.

Example:

You find that many companies in software development struggle with cloud integration. You could ask: "What challenges have you encountered with cloud integration as your data needs have grown?"

3. Implication Questions: Highlighting the Impact

Purpose:

To highlight the consequences of their problems. These questions bring urgency to finding a solution.

Examples:

"How does this issue affect your overall productivity?"

"What impact do these challenges have on your team's performance?"

Tips:

Use these questions to illustrate the severity of inaction. Help the client realize the cost of not solving their problem.

Be ready with scenario-based questions that show potential consequences.

Example:

In manufacturing, downtime equals revenue loss. You could ask: "How does system downtime affect your production schedules and revenue targets?"

4. Need-Payoff Questions: Demonstrating Value

Purpose: To help the client see the benefits of solving the problem. These questions guide them to envision a positive future with your solution.

Examples:

"How would a more efficient system improve your workflow?"
"What benefits would you see if this issue were resolved?"
Tips:
Focus on positive outcomes. Let the client imagine the improvements your solution will bring.
Use data, case studies and testimonials to demonstrate the success of your solution.
Example:
You have data showing another client improved efficiency by 25%. You ask: "If you could improve project turnaround time by 25%, how would this impact client satisfaction?"

By mastering the SPIN technique, you'll be able to craft a compelling narrative that resonates with Western clients, focusing on their core needs while building trust through clear, solution-driven dialogue. The more effectively you ask and respond, the closer you'll be to sealing the deal.

> **General Preparation Strategy:** Before meeting with the client, prepare a question map that includes all categories of SPIN questions. Tailor these questions based on your research and hypothetical scenarios.

The SPIN technique has laid the groundwork by helping you understand your client's needs. Now, it's time to take the next step: clearly and effectively communicating the solution you're offering. At this stage, you should have a solid grasp of who you're selling to, and it's all about delivering your pitch with precision and impact.

STRONG

Oren Klaff's STRONG Method, from his book *Pitch Anything*, explains precisely how to communicate your offering clearly and effectively. It's an approach designed to structure your pitch in a way that grabs attention, keeps your audience hooked, and leads to a clear decision.

The **STRONG** framework—**Setting the Frame, Telling the Story, Revealing the Intrigue, Offering the Prize, Nailing the Hookpoint,** and **Getting a Decision**—is a roadmap for you to follow every time you present an argument or pitch an idea. Let's take a closer look at each step and how you can apply it.

S – Setting the Frame

Think of this as setting the stage. You want to take control of the conversation and guide how your client views the pitch. Western clients like clarity, and they respect confidence. Start by clearly stating your purpose, explaining who you are, and what value you're bringing to the table. This helps them know why they should listen to you right from the beginning.

For example: "Hi, I'm Raj from XYZ Technologies. Today, I'll show you how our SmartAnalytics software can save your company time and money by streamlining your data analysis. We've worked with Fortune 500 companies for over 15 years, delivering proven results. Over the next 20 minutes, I'll show you how we can do the same for your company."

Setting the frame like this instantly tells the client: You're credible. You're here to solve their problem. And you respect their time. It's direct, focused, and exactly what Western audiences expect.

T - Telling the Story

This is where you make your pitch come alive. People relate to real-life stories more than they relate to facts, so don't just list features—tell a story about how your product made a difference in a real-world situation.

Here's how: "Last year, we worked with a major construction firm that was struggling with delays and increasing costs. Their outdated project management system wasn't keeping up with their needs. We introduced TaskMaster, our project management tool, and within six months, they saw a 30% reduction in delays and saved over €1 million in costs."

By telling a story like this, you're not just selling a tool – you're showing how it transforms a business. It's relatable and easy for your client to see how your product might solve their own problems.

R - Revealing the Intrigue

Now that you've got their attention, you need to show them what makes your offer truly special. Western clients appreciate innovation and anything that can give them an edge, so focus on what sets your product apart.

For example: "TaskMaster isn't just another project management tool—it uses AI-driven predictive analytics to forecast delays and cost overruns well in advance. Imagine being able to catch a problem before it even happens. That's the kind of control and foresight we're offering."

By revealing these unique aspects, you keep your audience curious and eager to know more. The intrigue keeps the conversation going.

O - Offering the Prize

This is the moment when you present the value proposition in a way that makes the offer irresistible. For Western clients, the most important factor here is the **return on investment (ROI)**. They need to clearly understand how your product or service is going to save them money, improve efficiency, or deliver measurable results. If they believe that the ROI justifies the cost, they are far more likely to accept the price you're offering.

Here's how you frame it: "TaskMaster can reduce your project delays by 30% and cut costs by 20%. This isn't just about improving efficiency—it's about saving real money and boosting your bottom line. For example, one of our clients in the construction industry saved over €1 million in the first year alone, thanks to better resource allocation and real-time project management. The cost of implementing TaskMaster was more than covered by these savings."

Offer real numbers and specific benefits. **Western clients care about the data** – how much money will they save, how much time will they cut, and how will their business grow as a result of your product? If you can provide clear evidence that shows how your solution delivers measurable ROI, the price becomes a secondary consideration.

Tip: Reinforce the connection between the price and the long-term gains they will see from using your solution. For example, "While there is an initial investment, the long-term savings and efficiency gains will far outweigh the cost. This isn't just an expense—it's an investment that will pay for itself."

By focusing on the ROI and giving concrete examples, you show that your product is not just worth the price – it's a smart business decision that delivers lasting value.

N - *Nailing the Hookpoint*

Now, it's time to lock in their interest. Reinforce the key points and address any objections they might have. Western clients value transparency, so be upfront and clear.

For example: "I know switching to a new system might feel like a big leap, but we offer full training and 24/7 support. Our clients have found the transition easy and immediately beneficial. By acting now, you'll be able to see the results by the end of the next quarter."

By nailing the hook point, you're showing them why they need to act now—and giving them the confidence that they're making the right decision.

G - *Getting a Decision*

Finally, you want to guide them to a clear and simple decision. Western clients appreciate straightforwardness, so make the process easy for them. Offer clear next steps and create a sense of urgency, but without pressure.

For example: "Let's get started with a pilot project, tailored to your needs. We can schedule a follow-up next week to finalize the details and make sure everything's in place.

This makes it easy for them to say yes and move forward. The decision is clear, the next steps are simple, and the value is obvious.

Let's look at how **the STRONG method** can be applied in a professional setting, specifically when trying to persuade a colleague to support a decision. The following scenario illustrates how each step of the STRONG framework works in practice, helping to create a structured, compelling argument that leads to action.

Imagine you're Priya, a project manager at a tech firm in India, trying to convince a long-standing Western client, Mr. Smith, to upgrade their outdated technology. Mr. Smith has been using the same system for years and isn't keen on changing something that 'still works'.

Setting the Frame

"Good morning, Smith. I really appreciate you taking the time to meet today. I know the current system has served you well for years, and it's understandable to stick with what you know. But as your business continues to grow, I'd like to show you why moving to our new technology could be the right step forward, offering long-term efficiency without disrupting your current workflow."

Why it works: Priya acknowledges the client's attachment to the old system but immediately frames the conversation as a forward-thinking solution that respects the client's current processes.

Telling the Story

"Last year, one of our major clients, similar to your company, was in the same position—relying on an older system that they felt comfortable with. They were hesitant to upgrade because of potential downtime and training concerns. But after discussing their needs, we introduced them to our new system. Not only did it address their fears, but within the first six months, they saw a 25% reduction in operating costs and a huge improvement in their team's efficiency."

Why it works: This story offers a relatable example that mirrors Mr Smith's situation, creating a bridge between the old and new systems and showing clear benefits without pushing too hard.

Revealing the Intrigue

"What's particularly exciting about this new system is that it integrates seamlessly with your current operations. It uses AI to predict maintenance issues before they arise, which could save your team hours of troubleshooting. And the best part is that the transition is designed to be smooth, with little to no downtime."

Why it works: Priya highlights unique, innovative features that directly address the client's concerns—emphasizing how this transition won't be disruptive and will, in fact, solve specific problems Mr Smith didn't even realize were there.

Offering the Prize

"By making this switch, you're not just upgrading a tool—you're investing in future-proofing your business. You'll see faster workflows, fewer unexpected breakdowns, and reduced operational costs. Over time, we estimate you could save 15% annually on maintenance alone, with a full return on investment in under a year."

Why it works: Here, Priya focuses on the ultimate prize—ROI, efficiency, and long-term gains. This aligns perfectly with the Western client's focus on measurable results and benefits.

Nailing the Hookpoint

"I completely understand that making a change can feel risky, especially when the current system has worked for so long. But the reality is, staying with outdated technology could mean falling behind competitors who are already moving ahead with these newer tools. If you delay, the cost of catching up later could be far higher."

Getting a Decision

"Let's make this transition as easy as possible. I suggest we start with a pilot project. This way, you can see how the system works in one department before fully committing. Can we meet next week to finalize the details and get the pilot underway? I'm happy to answer any questions you have."

Setting expectation is one thing, delivering on them is everything

In this chapter, we've unlocked the essentials of convincing and selling to Western clients: focus on delivering clear, concise, and solution-driven communication. While personal connections matter, Western clients value efficiency and results over relationships when it comes to decision-making. To succeed, shift your attention from relationship-building to presenting a pitch that highlights measurable value, backed by data and a solid return on investment.

As discussed in the chapter on time, time is money in the West. Use the SPIN framework to deeply understand your client's needs before the meeting, and let the STRONG method guide you through a confident, results-focused pitch. The more clearly and directly you present solutions, the more credibility you'll build, showing that you understand their problems and can solve them effectively.

As an Indian working with Western clients, you likely offer a pricing advantage compared to Western competition—that's your key competitive edge. However, all of your competitors in India offer the same advantage: lower prices. So how do you stand out? Don't focus only on the price; instead, demonstrate the skills you've gained from this book. You don't need to mention that you've taken a course or read a book—just show them through your actions. Tell your clients that you value time, clear communication, openness, and collaboration. Let them know that you'll be proactive in finding solutions together. If they believe these values are naturally part of how you work, they'll choose you over the competition without hesitation. But remember—setting expectations is one thing, delivering on them is everything.

Lastly, it's not about who you know, your background, or your family—that does not matter—it's one hundred percent about what you can deliver. Whether you're pitching to a CEO or a junior associate, your ability to communicate will set you apart. As we head into the next chapter, we'll dive into the nuances of hierarchy in Western business culture and how to tailor your approach to resonate at all levels of the organization.

---

*Skill 6: Effectively **convince** by delivering clear, concise, and solution-focused arguments to establish credibility.*

Exercise: The 3-Step Persuasion Practice

For your next request or proposal to a Western colleague or client, try this 3-step approach to improve clarity and impact. Notice their response, and adjust your style based on what resonates. **Objective:** Practice clear, solution-focused persuasion.

1. **State Your Point in One Sentence:** Start with a clear, specific sentence about what you need or suggest. For example, "I recommend we try [solution] to improve [goal]."

2. **Explain the Solution's Value:** Briefly explain *why* this helps. Skip the process details—focus on the result. Example: "This approach will streamline our workflow."

3. **Highlight a Measurable Benefit:** Conclude with a clear benefit, like, "This will save us 3 hours weekly."

7

Kick Upwards: Engaging with Superiors Confidently

❧❋❧

How to embrace direct communication with leaders and build credibility across levels.

To earn respect from Western managers, challenge upwards and show independence—don't wait for instructions; identify and propose tasks yourself.

Lost in Translation

In the heart of Bangalore, Rajesh Kumar had just embarked on an exciting new journey as the lead consultant for a Norwegian tech company. With over a decade of experience in the IT sector in India, he felt confident in his abilities and eager to prove himself.

His journey began with a virtual meeting with his new boss, Lars Andersen. Lars was well-known for his innovative mindset and egalitarian leadership style. Right from the start, he made it clear that he valued open communication, direct feedback, and a collaborative environment where every voice mattered.

"Call me Lars," he said with a friendly smile during their first video call. "We don't stand on ceremony here. I want you to participate in discussions, share your ideas freely, and make decisions as you see fit."

Rajesh, who had never worked with anyone from the West before, was taken aback. Used to the more hierarchical structure of Indian companies, where deference to superiors was expected, this new approach felt foreign. In India, addressing a superior by their first name and making decisions without approval was not normal. Rajesh nodded politely, but the cultural shift that Lars expected would take more than just a smile to adopt.

In the weeks that followed, Rajesh focused on his assignments diligently, always double-checking with Lars before making any decisions. He addressed him as 'Sir' in emails and meetings, waiting for directives instead of offering his own input. Lars noticed this but hoped Rajesh would eventually adjust to the more egalitarian culture.

Then came a pivotal moment. During a key project meeting, the team was discussing a critical decision about software implementation. Lars, as usual, encouraged everyone to share their views. Rajesh, despite having valuable insights, remained silent, unsure if it was his place to speak. The meeting ended without Rajesh contributing, and he knew that the decision made wasn't the best possible one.

Afterwards, in a one-on-one call, Lars addressed the situation. "Rajesh, I noticed you didn't share your thoughts in the meeting. We really value your expertise, and we need you to contribute actively."

Rajesh, feeling as though he had disappointed Lars, apologized. "I'm sorry, Sir. I didn't want to overstep my bounds."

Lars sighed, realizing the extent of the cultural disconnect. "Rajesh, here in Norway, we work as equals. I need you to be assertive and proactive."

Despite this conversation, Rajesh found it difficult to break free from the habits ingrained by years of experience in a hierarchical system. In meetings, he continued to defer to Lars and senior colleagues, seeking approval for even minor decisions. His emails remained formal, filled with honorifics and careful language, which stood out against the direct and informal communication style of his Norwegian counterparts.

Lars's frustration grew. The Norwegian team, used to making decisions quickly and independently, found Rajesh's constant deference and need for approval to be cumbersome. The efficiency Lars had envisioned from their collaboration was being lost in translation.

The situation came to a head during a high-stakes project. Rajesh, tasked with implementing a crucial software update, hesitated to move forward without explicit approval from Lars. He sent a detailed email outlining his plan and waited for a response. But Lars, tied up with other priorities, didn't see the email right away.

By the time Lars got back to him, valuable time had been wasted, and the project was delayed. In a tense follow-up meeting, Lars's frustration surfaced. "Rajesh, we can't afford these delays. You need to make decisions on your own. This micromanagement isn't working."

Rajesh was left feeling guilty and confused. All his life, he had believed that respecting hierarchy and seeking approval were signs of professionalism. But now, this experience was challenging everything.

Kick upwards and praise downwards

If you've ever felt uncertain about how to approach your boss in a Western work environment or wondered whether it's okay to challenge their ideas, you're not alone. Rajesh's story is far from unique—it's something many experience when transitioning from a traditional, hierarchy-driven workplace to one that values openness and direct communication. And believe me, this can be one of the biggest cultural hurdles when it comes to working with the West.

In this chapter, I want to help you feel more comfortable with these moments of uncertainty. I'm going to show you how to confidently navigate conversations with your superiors and embrace the Western approach to hierarchy. In India, you're probably used to well-defined structures where respect for authority is deeply ingrained. But in the West, the workplace hierarchy is much flatter, and autonomy is not just expected—it's respected.

Now, I know this shift can feel intimidating at first. You might think, "But I don't want to come across as disrespectful." That's completely natural. But here's the thing: being assertive and taking initiative doesn't mean you're undermining authority—it means you're being **recognized** for your **ideas and contributions**. It's a different kind of respect, one that's built on collaboration and trust.

Let me tell you about an experience I had during my time at one of the big four consultancy firms. I watched an Indian consultant go from being just another team member to gaining the trust of a Norwegian partner, not because of his technical skills alone, but because he wasn't afraid to speak up. He pushed for more control over a project, communicated clearly and confidently, and earned the respect of his superior. It aligns perfectly with the advice that my grandfather once told me that has stuck with me my whole career: **always kick upwards and praise downwards.**

Reflection point: Are you comfortable disagreeing with your manager?

That's the key takeaway here. If you're only following orders, you might be seen as someone who lacks initiative and is just one of the pack, a follower. But if you assert yourself and share your insights—even when it feels risky—you'll become a valuable asset, someone your team can't do without. It's about finding that balance: respecting your superiors while still having the courage to stand up and make your voice heard. That's the path to true professional respect and recognition.

The Roots of Indian Hierarchies

To truly understand the hierarchical structure of Indian workplaces, we have to take a step back and look at the foundation it's built on—families. In India, the family isn't just a support system; it's the bedrock of society, and it operates on a clear, deeply respected hierarchy. From a young age, you are probably taught that respect for elders is non-negotiable. Major decisions are often made by the most senior family members, and questioning their authority? That's almost unheard of.

Think about your own family for a moment. In a typical Indian household, roles and responsibilities are carefully assigned based on age, and sometimes even gender. Fathers, grandfathers, and other elder figures hold the highest authority, and their word often becomes law. This isn't just about keeping order—it's a way of showing reverence for the wisdom that comes with age.

This respect for hierarchy that we learn at home naturally carries over into the workplace. It's easy to see why many Indian employees view their bosses in much the same way they view their elders—figures of authority who are not to be questioned. The idea of challenging a superior or making an independent decision without first consulting them often feels unnatural, even wrong.

In Speaking of India, Craig Storti delves into the hierarchical dynamics deeply embedded in Indian workplaces, which mirror the hierarchy found within Indian families. Just as family elders are respected and rarely questioned, bosses in Indian companies often occupy a similar role, where loyalty, obedience, and respect are paramount. This paternalistic management fosters strong loyalty but also reinforces a top-down system where decisions flow from the top, and questioning authority is rare.

The challenge comes when Indian professionals step into a Western work environment, where the rules are different. Hierarchy is flatter, and employees are expected to take ownership of decisions, be assertive, and collaborate openly. Traits that may have helped you succeed in a traditional Indian corporate setting—deference to authority, careful avoidance of disagreement—will be misinterpreted as hesitation or lack of initiative in a Western context.

Craig Storti points out in his book Speaking of India that the surest way to win favor in an Indian work environment is never to offend or disagree with those above you. Simply put, those who enjoy the boss's favor thrive, while those who do not struggle. The key to gaining this favor is to avoid offending or disagreeing with superiors at all costs. In other words, protecting the face of one's superior is paramount.

As a reader, you might be resistant to challenging your boss with any of the following actions:

- Challenge or question something the boss says.
- Disagree with something the boss says.

- Correct the boss in front of others.
- Act as if you know more than your boss.
- Criticize, even by implication, something the boss says or does.
- Answer a question (by someone else) in front of the boss.
- Fail to inform the boss about something.
- Make even a routine decision without informing the boss.

The first three actions – challenging, questioning, and disagreeing with your boss – need to be done in all cultures as part of normal business. However, in Indian culture, these actions are rarely done in front of others and never overtly. Indians tend to handle these situations very indirectly, as discussed in the chapter on communication.

In contrast, in many Western work environments, thriving often requires the total opposite: disagreeing, correcting, and making independent decisions without always asking for permission. However, there is a delicate balance between going too far and not doing enough.

However, while these traditional structures remain deeply embedded in many Indian workplaces, times are changing. Particularly among younger professionals, there's a noticeable shift toward more egalitarian values. This new generation, influenced by multinational corporations, tech startups, and the rise of digital work environments, favors collaboration, open dialogue, and shared decision-making. They are more comfortable voicing their opinions and expect to work in environments where their ideas are heard and valued.

Foundations of Egalitarian Leadership

To understand why Western workplaces have developed flatter and more egalitarian structures, it's crucial to explore the broader social, economic, and cultural changes that have shaped these societies over time. The West's shift away from rigid hierarchies stems from several key factors, all of which have influenced modern workplace dynamics.

Historically, medieval European society was as hierarchical as it gets. Kings, nobles, and peasants lived within a strict social order, and this structure naturally extended into work environments where leaders had unquestioned authority. Factories during the Industrial Revolution of the 18th and 19th centuries maintained these top-down systems, but with a growing focus on efficiency and productivity. While workers were still expected to follow orders without question, this era marked the beginning of more formalized management systems.

The early 20th century brought 'scientific management', introduced by Frederick Winslow Taylor, which aimed to improve productivity by dividing labor between managers (who planned) and workers (who executed). This model, while effective for a time, eventually showed its limitations. The rigid hierarchy stifled creativity and made workers feel like mere cogs in a machine, disconnected from the decision-making process.

Then came a profound shift. By the 1930s and 1940s, thinkers like Elton Mayo and Abraham Maslow began emphasizing the importance of worker satisfaction and social needs. They found that happy, engaged workers were far more productive than those simply following orders. This discovery sparked the Human Relations Movement, which encouraged flatter, more collaborative work environments where managers engaged directly with employees and valued their input.

The post-World War II boom accelerated this transformation. The rise of the knowledge economy, where ideas and information became central to success, demanded workplaces that fostered creativity and innovation. Rigid hierarchies, with their slow decision-making processes, were increasingly seen as obstacles to progress. Companies like Google and Apple later epitomized this shift, creating work environments where even junior employees could challenge ideas, contribute solutions, and drive innovation.

Western society's broader cultural shift toward individualism also played a significant role. Unlike in traditional hierarchical societies, the West began to place greater emphasis on individual rights and personal autonomy, a shift rooted in the Enlightenment era of the 17th and 18th centuries. As people moved away from family-centric roles and became more economically independent, individual merit started to outweigh social status. This ethos of self-reliance and independence shaped not only social relationships but also workplace dynamics, fostering a culture where employees were empowered to take initiative and make decisions.

The social movements of the 1960s and 1970s—civil rights, feminism, and labor rights—further propelled the shift toward equality and inclusivity. These movements helped dismantle hierarchical structures in society and brought these values into the workplace, advocating for more egalitarian practices where everyone had a voice, regardless of rank.

Today, Western workplaces reflect these historical shifts through agile methodologies, teamwork, and flexible decision-making structures. The rise of remote work and digital tools has only reinforced the need for adaptable, fast-moving organizations. Rigid hierarchies are increasingly seen as impediments to success in a world that values innovation and speed. The modern Western workplace thrives on the contributions of every employee, from the newest recruit to the senior executive, creating an environment where collaboration and open communication are key to staying competitive.

Benefits of Flat Hierarchies from a Western Perspective

Henry Mintzberg is a renowned Canadian academic and author in the field of management and organizational theory. He defines flat hierarchy as:

"Few levels of hierarchy, decentralization of decision-making, and reliance on mutual adjustment among people. This type of structure fosters flexibility, responsiveness, and the ability to adapt quickly to changing circumstances."

According to Mintzberg, flat hierarchies can be understood through the following key features:

Minimal Levels of Middle Management: Flat hierarchies reduce the number of managerial layers between the top executives and the frontline employees, promoting more direct communication and quicker decision-making.

Decentralized Decision-Making: Decision-making authority is distributed throughout the organization, rather than being concentrated at the top. This allows employees at various levels to take initiative and make decisions relevant to their work.

Organic Structure: Flat hierarchies are more organic compared to mechanistic structures. This means they are more flexible, adaptive, and rely on informal communication channels rather than rigid protocols.

Employee Empowerment: By having fewer levels of management, employees are given more responsibility and autonomy, which can lead to increased motivation and job satisfaction.

Enhanced Collaboration: With fewer hierarchical barriers, flat organizations encourage more collaboration and interaction among employees, fostering a more integrated and cooperative work environment.

As we've explored the differences in hierarchies between Indian and Western workplaces, it's key to understand why flatter structures have become so widespread, especially in industries driven by innovation and speed.

Consider innovation. In a company like Zappos, employees don't need to navigate layers of approval to share ideas. This openness encourages creativity and gives people the confidence to propose bold solutions. By empowering employees to contribute freely, Zappos saw a dramatic increase in the flow of innovative ideas. The result? Fresh solutions that may have otherwise been buried in a rigid structure.

Then there's employee satisfaction. Research supports this: companies with engaged employees—those empowered to act—tend to outperform their competitors. In fact, a Gallup survey found that these companies enjoy up to 21% higher profitability. It's not just about autonomy; it's about fostering a sense of ownership and responsibility that drives employees to excel.

Let's not forget flexibility. In industries where agility is a necessity, flatter structures help companies respond quickly to changes without getting bogged down by multiple layers of decision-makers. A study from the Harvard Business Review found that organizations with decentralized structures could adapt more swiftly to market disruptions, offering a crucial competitive edge.

Remember, it's not about one approach being better than the other; it's about understanding the Western view of why we value this type. Western leaders sometimes struggle when they impose their flat leadership style in Indian workplaces, just as Indian professionals can find Western systems disorienting. The key takeaway is that you shouldn't wait for managers to give you all the instructions. It's a collaborative process—they may provide some guidance, but often, you'll need to carve out your own path and confirm it with them.

Avoid Misunderstanding

When Indian professionals step into Western work environments, it's easy for misunderstandings to arise if they're unsure about how hierarchies work in the West. I've witnessed this firsthand through comments from my own Western colleagues. Their frustration wasn't due to a lack of competence from our Indian counterparts but because of cultural differences that weren't fully understood.

The problem of misunderstanding often stems from misaligned expectations. Below is a general comparison of expectations between Western and Indian managers:

Western Managers: They value independence and active contribution. They expect you to identify your own tasks and solutions. If you're unsure or face challenges, they anticipate that you will proactively raise issues rather than waiting for them to follow up. Consequently, they tend to monitor progress less closely.

Indian Managers: They typically follow a top-down approach. They assign tasks, expecting employees to adhere to the instructions and patterns they've outlined. Indian managers are more likely to monitor progress closely and actively check in throughout the workday.

Understanding the expectations of the manager you're working with is crucial. If you anticipate an Indian-style approach but encounter the more hands-off Western approach, the resulting misalignment can lead to frustration. To avoid this, it's essential to align expectations. I encourage you to establish an open dialogue at the start of any project to clarify your manager's expectations and adjust your approach accordingly.

In Western companies, the expectation is often for more independence, quicker decision-making, and assertiveness. These differences can lead to a series of challenges—missed opportunities, inefficiencies, and even strained relationships. Below, I've outlined common negative outcomes that can arise when these cultural differences aren't fully navigated. By understanding them, we can take steps to bridge the gap and foster smoother collaboration.

- Loss of Valuable Insights: Key ideas and suggestions go unheard because Indian professionals hesitate to share openly in a flat hierarchy, fearing it may be seen as overstepping.
- Missed Growth Opportunities: Waiting for approval or recognition can mean that proactive Western colleagues advance more quickly, leaving Indian employees overlooked despite their competence.
- Misunderstanding of Skills: Western teams' hesitancy to assert ideas or take independent action may lead them to underestimate an Indian professional's skills or capabilities.

- Reduced Efficiency: Delays occur when Indian employees defer decisions to superiors, resulting in slower project timelines compared to the fast-paced decision-making expected in Western companies.
- Stifled Innovation: A reluctance to challenge ideas or offer creative solutions directly can limit innovation within teams that rely on open, collaborative idea-sharing.
- Frustration from Western Colleagues: Western counterparts may grow frustrated with perceived micromanagement or the need for constant approval, leading to strained team dynamics.
- Over-reliance on Hierarchy: Indian employees might feel uncomfortable taking initiative without guidance, leading to bottlenecks and delays in project progress when supervisors are unavailable.
- Trust Issues: Western colleagues may perceive hesitancy to act independently as a lack of confidence, resulting in diminished trust in an Indian professional's capabilities.

The beauty of the misunderstandings above is that you hold the key to avoiding their outcomes. Simply by being aware of them, you gain a crucial advantage. Understanding how these dynamics play out places you inside the mind of your Western counterparts, enabling you to navigate situations more effectively and prevent these cultural missteps before they happen. With this awareness, you can turn potential challenges into opportunities for stronger, more productive relationships.

Navigating Do's and Don'ts

Navigating the balance between independence and deference in a Western work environment can be challenging but rewarding.

Understanding when to act independently and when to consult your superior is crucial for fostering trust and ensuring effective collaboration. Even though this chapter has so far been focused on independence and making decisions yourself, there are times when you need to consult with your superior before making a decision. This balance is essential for leveraging the freedom and responsibility that come with a flat hierarchical structure.

Finding the Sweet Spot: Independence vs. Consultation

When working in a Western environment, it's crucial to understand the balance between taking initiative and knowing when to seek approval. A good starting point is always to ask your superior where the boundaries of decision-making lie. This initial conversation will give you clarity about your autonomy. If you're ever in doubt, it's best to ask for guidance, but remember that once you understand the limits, you don't need to seek approval for similar decisions in the future.

Your level of decision-making authority is also linked to the trust you've built with your superior. The more trust you establish over time, the more autonomy you'll earn in making decisions independently. Below are guidelines to help you determine when to act on your own and when to involve your superior.

When to Make Decisions Independently:
- **Routine and Operational Decisions:** If the decision is routine and falls within your scope of responsibilities, especially if it aligns with established company policies, go ahead. Handling routine decisions on your own shows you can manage your role without constant oversight.
- **Small-Scale, Low-Risk Decisions:** For low-risk decisions with minimal impact on other departments, taking the initiative is encouraged. For example, approving a minor expense within your budget or adjusting team schedules.

- **Expertise-Driven Choices:** When the decision is within your area of expertise and you have the necessary information, feel confident to act. Using your specialized knowledge demonstrates competence and strengthens your role.

When to Consult Your Superior:
- **Strategic and High-Impact Decisions:** Consult your superior for decisions with significant impact on the company's direction, budget, or reputation. This includes major financial commitments, strategic shifts, or decisions that affect company resources.
- **Cross-Departmental Impacts:** If your decision will impact other teams or departments, involve your superior and relevant stakeholders to ensure coordination. This prevents conflicts and supports broader organizational goals.
- **Ambiguity and Uncertainty:** In situations where guidelines are unclear or you're navigating unfamiliar territory, it's wise to seek advice. Consulting your superior helps prevent potential missteps and ensures alignment with the company's strategic vision.

There isn't a definite line on when to consult and when to act independently, but the key takeaway is this: avoid asking about every minor detail. Instead, **approach your superior with a proposed solution.** This shows initiative and **positions you as a problem** solver rather than someone **who waits for instructions.**

Raising Your Voice: When and How to Disagree

Disagreeing with your boss, especially if you're used to a culture of deference, might seem like stepping into unfamiliar territory. However, as you continue working with the West, you'll need to embrace a different mindset—one where offering constructive disagreement is not just accepted but expected. In many Western workplaces, questioning and challenging ideas are part of the daily workflow. It's a sign that you're engaged, invested in the outcome, and thinking critically about the best path forward.

When I worked with Peter, the managing partner at one of the big four consultancy firms, I quickly learned that challenging his ideas wasn't just encouraged; it was essential. Peter was the type of leader who valued independent thought, but he didn't give in easily. His convictions were strong, and if you questioned him, you had to come prepared with well-founded arguments. Every debate was rigorous, and I'll admit, it wasn't easy. But that was the key to earning his respect. Those who took the easier route of staying silent, nodding in agreement, or avoiding confrontation altogether found themselves fading into the background, their contributions forgotten.

So, how do you approach disagreement in a Western setting in a way that ensures your input is valued rather than dismissed? Let's break it down.

First, timing is crucial. It's not about when you disagree, but how and where you do it. Think of it this way: public challenges in a high-pressure meeting? Probably not the best idea. Instead, pick your moment. A private conversation or a smaller project team discussion can set the right tone for a constructive dialogue.

Next, you have to build your case. It's not enough to simply say you disagree—you need solid evidence to back it up. In Western workplaces, data and concrete facts carry a lot of weight. If you've spotted an issue with a project or have a better way of doing something, lay out your reasoning clearly and make sure your point is supported by facts or real examples. The key is to show that your argument is grounded in thorough analysis, not just gut feeling.

And here's an important one: make it about the solution, not just the problem. When you raise a concern or challenge a decision, always have a constructive alternative in mind. This shows that you're not just pointing out flaws but also thinking proactively about how to improve the situation. It's a huge shift from simply deferring to a boss's authority— you're now positioning yourself as a problem solver, someone who cares about the outcome as much as they do.

Remember, being respectful doesn't mean you have to tiptoe around the issue. It's about presenting your argument in a way that acknowledges the other person's perspective while confidently sharing your own. You might start by saying something like, "I see where you're coming from, but I've noticed a few things that might change the outcome, and I'd love to discuss them."

Examples of how you might start a conversation to express a differing opinion:

- Seeking Clarification Approach: "I'd like to understand your perspective on [topic] better. Could you walk me through your reasoning? I have some thoughts that might add to our approach, but I want to make sure I fully understand your position first."

- Common Ground Approach: "I really appreciate the direction we're taking with [project or decision]. I've been thinking about how we can make it even more effective, and I have a suggestion I'd like to discuss that could align well with our goals."

- Feedback Request Approach: "Could we review the plans for [specific task or project]? I've been reviewing the details and might have some feedback that could help us optimize the process."
- Constructive Alternative Approach: "I've been reflecting on what we discussed in our last meeting about [subject]. There are some potential challenges I see with the current approach, and I'd like to propose an alternative for us to consider. When is a good time for us to sit down and talk about this?"
- Respectful Challenge Approach: "You've outlined a clear vision for [specific issue or project], and while I see the strengths in this plan, there are aspects that concern me. Could we set aside some time to explore these concerns together? I believe there might be a few adjustments that could really enhance our outcomes."

Step-by-Step Guide on How to Adapt to Western Hierarchies

Adapting to Western hierarchies can feel like a significant shift, but it's a transition that will greatly enhance your effectiveness in less rigid work environments. To help you navigate this change smoothly, here's a step-by-step guide tailored to those making the adjustment:

Step 1: Understand the Structure

Research the Company: Before starting your new role, take time to study the company's organizational structure. While there may be fewer layers of hierarchy, it's still crucial to understand the chain of command and how decisions flow within the company.

Observe Interactions: Once you're in the role, pay close attention to how people communicate with their superiors and colleagues. Notice how decisions are made and how employees contribute ideas during meetings.

Step 2: Embrace Informality

Use First Names: In many Western workplaces, formality takes a backseat. You're likely to be encouraged to address everyone, including senior leadership, by their first names. Embrace this as a sign of mutual respect and collegiality.

Open Dialogue: Be prepared to contribute actively in discussions. Western companies value open communication, where employees at all levels are expected to share their thoughts and opinions freely.

Step 3: Initiate Communication

Be Proactive: Don't wait for instructions. If you see an area where you can contribute or have a question, take the initiative to address it. Being proactive in Western workplaces is seen as a sign of engagement and is expected.

Seek and Offer Feedback: Regular feedback is common in Western work culture, and it's seen as a way to improve. Be open to receiving it, but don't hesitate to provide feedback in return. It fosters an environment of continuous improvement.

Step 4: Show Initiative

Problem-Solving: Show your independence by tackling challenges head-on. Offering solutions, not just identifying problems, demonstrates your commitment and capacity for independent thinking.

Decision-Making: Get comfortable with making decisions within your area of expertise. Taking ownership of decisions signals confidence and helps build trust with your team and leadership.

* * *

Kick-upwards

As we reflect on Rajesh Kumar's experience from early in this chapter, his story reminds us of the nuances involved in navigating cultural differences in the workplace. His transition from a hierarchical Indian environment to a more egalitarian Western company was not without its challenges, but it underscores a critical lesson: adaptability is key to thriving in global business. Working across cultures requires more than adjusting to different hierarchies—it demands openness, flexibility, and a willingness to embrace new perspectives. For Indian professionals entering Western work environments, success lies in understanding that assertiveness, autonomy, and direct communication are valued. It's about having the courage to say your true opinions out loud, regardless of who you talk to.

Rajesh's journey was about more than survival—it was about growth. And for you, it can be the same. By embracing new ways of working and stepping outside of your comfort zone, you not only elevate your professional journey but also create opportunities for deeper collaboration and innovation.

But where do you get the chance to make your voice heard and leave an impact? The answer is simple: **meetings**. Meetings are more than formalities – they're the battlegrounds for ideas, influence, and recognition in the West. In the next chapter, we'll explore how to turn meetings into your greatest tool for success. We'll dive into how mastering this environment can propel your career forward.

I end this chapter with a dedication to my grandpa, with his quote that will follow me forever, *"Kick upwards, that's how you get recognition in the corporate world."*

Skill 7: *Comfortably engage in direct conversations with superiors and embrace the cultural emphasis on egalitarianism and open communication across levels.*

Exercise: *Mapping the Hierarchy and Understanding Roles*

Objective: Develop a clear understanding of the structure and expectations within a Western hierarchy, where hierarchy may feel less formal but is still present and influential.

1. **Research the Structure:** Start by mapping out your team or organization. Identify who reports to whom, noting any informal leaders or influential colleagues who aren't necessarily higher in rank but play a key role in decision-making. This will help you understand the Western emphasis on role function over rank alone. If you are working virtually with a Western client, call a colleague and have a discussion on the point above with him/her.

2. **Observe Communication Styles:** For one week, pay close attention to how your colleagues interact with managers and leaders. Look for differences in how they communicate with senior leaders compared to peers, noting any respectful informality, directness, or openness.

If you are working virtually with a Western client, call a colleague and have a discussion on point 1 and 2 above with him/her.

3. **Practice Direct Communication:** Choose a small task or project update to practice being direct. Approach your manager or a senior colleague with a brief update, and focus on being clear, concise, and straightforward—without additional formality or deference.

4. **Craft Your Own Assignment:** Before receiving instructions from your manager, take the initiative to define your own task or project based on your understanding of team priorities. Outline the problem, propose a solution, and

draft a brief plan of action. Once complete, share your proposed assignment with your manager for feedback and confirmation. This exercise will help you develop independence and demonstrate initiative, key traits valued in Western work environments.

8

Own the Room: Expressing Opinions and Participating in Decisions

❧❋❧

Become comfortable with sharing your voice and actively shaping discussions.

The conference room at GlobalTech was more than just a meeting space—it was a melting pot of cultures. On one side, Arjun and Priya, seasoned professionals from India, had prepared for what they viewed as a routine, formal session. Meanwhile, Mark and Susan, their U.S. counterparts, saw it as an interactive forum for collaboration, a place to debate ideas and make real-time decisions. The goal for the day was to finalize the design for a new software interface. But it quickly became apparent that this meeting was going to surface more than just design considerations.

Arjun began the meeting with a summary of the project's progress. *"We've reached a consensus on the overall design of the interface,"* he announced, his smile warm but formal. *"Today, we'll present the decisions we've made."*

Mark, eager to engage, leaned in. *"Great! Let's dive into the details. Everyone here is an equal participant, so please share your views freely."* His tone was casual, encouraging a flow of ideas.

Priya nodded in agreement and continued, *"We've outlined the key features. The main dashboard will include user metrics, notifications, and quick access to support."*

Not one to wait, Mark jumped in with a suggestion. *"What if we integrate user feedback directly into the dashboard? Susan, what do you think?"*

Susan chimed in, *"Absolutely, that could be a valuable addition."*

Arjun paused, hesitating. *"We can look into that,"* he replied, intending to discuss it later with Priya in private. He glanced at her, and with a subtle shake of her head, she signaled that they should stick to their prepared agenda.

As the meeting progressed, Mark and Susan continued to offer suggestions and feedback, viewing the meeting as an opportunity to brainstorm and make decisions on the spot. Arjun and Priya, however, saw it as a setting to present what had already been discussed in one-on-one conversations, not a place to make changes in real-time.

At one point, Mark proposed a major change to the user interface layout. *"I believe this new layout will improve the user experience. What do you think, Arjun?"*

Again, Arjun smiled politely. *"We can discuss this in more detail after the meeting."*

Slightly puzzled, Mark responded, *"Now's a good time, while everyone's here."*

Priya interjected, her tone gentle but firm. *"We think certain aspects of your suggestion need further consideration. Let's have a focused discussion later."*

During a break, Mark turned to Susan. *"It feels like we're not getting anywhere. They keep deferring the discussion."*

Susan nodded. *"I noticed. It's as if they don't want to engage directly during the meeting."*

Meanwhile, Arjun and Priya used the break to strategize. *"We need to address their concerns without causing conflict,"* Priya said. *"We'll talk to them one-on-one afterwards."*

When they reconvened, the same dynamic played out. Mark raised a point about the project timeline. *"We're a bit behind schedule. How do we catch up?"*

Arjun replied diplomatically, *"We're aware of the timeline and are taking steps to meet our deadlines."*

Seeking more clarity, Mark asked, *"Can you specify what steps?"*

Priya, maintaining her calm demeanor, answered, *"We're coordinating with our team to streamline the processes."*

Mark and Susan exchanged glances, still not getting the transparency they were used to. Nevertheless, they decided to let the meeting unfold and adapt.

As the meeting drew to a close, Arjun summarized, *"We've noted all the points raised and will address them in our next discussions."*

Mark, still feeling a disconnect, said, *"Let's schedule another meeting soon to finalize these details."*

Priya smiled warmly, *"Yes, let's plan for that. We'll come prepared with our responses."*

In the world of global business, meetings are where ideas take shape, strategies are debated, and decisions are made. Yet, when professionals from different cultures come together in these forums, misunderstandings, subtle tensions, and missed opportunities can easily arise.

For you, an Indian professional navigating Western corporate spaces, mastering the art of meetings is more than just learning how to contribute—it's about understanding what's happening beneath the surface. Western meetings, unlike those in more hierarchical environments, are arenas where directness, quick exchanges, and active participation are key. But here's the twist: it's not just about speaking up. There are unwritten rules and cues that shape how your ideas will be received.

By the end of this chapter, you'll uncover these hidden dynamics and learn how to thrive in Western meetings—not by conforming completely, but by leveraging your strengths to collaborate more effectively. Every chapter in this book builds on the importance of direct, face-to-face interaction with your Western colleagues. In most cases, the only real opportunities for this come during meetings, so it's crucial to make the most of them for your future success.

A new approach to meeting – moving away from 'harmony'.

> **Reflection point:** Think about the meetings you attended last week. What were the objectives and purposes of those meetings, and how did you contribute to them?

How meetings are conducted varies based on culture. There's no absolute right or wrong, but when working with a Western company, it's crucial to know how they operate. If you're unaware of their norms, excelling at your job alone may not be enough. In Western workplaces, much of what is perceived as excellence is showcased in meetings. Whether you like it or not, meetings are one of the key arenas where you can demonstrate your skills and insights. In many cases, especially in fields like consulting, what you contribute during meetings is often as important, if not more so, than the actual work you do. Meetings are where your superiors and clients hear your thoughts, reflections, and ideas.

In India, meetings are often about maintaining harmony. They typically serve as a space to present decisions that have already been agreed upon in private conversations. Major disagreements or issues are often handled outside the meeting room, where one-on-one discussions take place beforehand. In meetings, attendees tend to focus on finalizing finer points, while any contentious issues are deferred for private resolution. Frequent breaks are used to quietly manage new obstacles, and smaller group discussions often take place to finalize decisions after the larger meeting has concluded.

You might recognize some of the points below as things that are considered almost *off-limits* in your *normal* meetings:

1. Disagreeing with what someone else says.
2. Correcting someone who is presenting.
3. Criticizing a colleague or superior.
4. Challenging something said during the meeting.
5. Making overtly negative comments about someone.
6. Giving negative feedback.
7. Saying that something isn't possible.
8. Admitting a mistake.
9. Confessing that you didn't understand something.
10. Acknowledging that you're behind schedule or unlikely to meet a deadline.
11. Asking for help or more time.

However, in the West, these points are not just acceptable—they're often appreciated. In Western settings, it's expected that you'll have your own opinions, offer suggestions, participate actively, and think independently.

Purpose of Meeting in the West

In Western workplaces, meetings are a chance to truly shine. They aren't just about checking boxes or going through the motions – they're one of the most important places where you can show your value. If you're not familiar with the Western style of meetings, it can feel a little strange at first. It's less about presenting decisions already made and more about openly discussing ideas, solving problems, and making decisions together. This is where a lot of the 'real work' gets done.

Imagine this: You walk into a meeting at a Western tech company, expecting a formal, structured discussion with managers taking the lead on giving instructions. What happens instead? The meeting turns into a buzzing hive of ideas, a dynamic exchange where even the most junior member's opinion holds weight. That's the hallmark of meetings in the West—collaboration, open dialogue, and problem-solving in real-time. To succeed, you need to know the purpose behind these meetings. Let's break it down into multiple layers and purposes of meetings.

Next Steps: Mapping the Path Forward

The team's goal for this meeting? Figuring out exactly who is doing what. You'll often hear phrases like, *"What's next?"* or *"Who's owning this?"* By the end, every participant knows their role, what tasks they're handling, and the deadlines. Clear, simple, and effective.

Brainstorming: Where Ideas Collide

Meetings are the birthplace of innovation. Picture a whiteboard covered in scribbles and diagrams. Everyone is pitching their wildest ideas, and no one holds back. This collaborative environment sparks the kind of creative thinking that leads to breakthroughs.

Checking Progress: Are We On Track?

At regular intervals, meetings provide a pulse check. Are you hitting deadlines? What's holding you back? These moments are essential for identifying roadblocks and finding ways to overcome them together.

Presenting Ideas: Refining the Rough Edges

Maybe you've got a new feature idea, or you've identified an area for improvement. Here's your chance to present, and more importantly, receive feedback. In these meetings, group input turns rough ideas into polished strategies.

Supporting Junior Members: Where Growth Happens

In Western meetings, senior leaders are not the only ones who talk. Junior members are encouraged to speak up, share challenges, and seek advice. These moments provide mentorship opportunities that help younger professionals grow.

Collaborative Decision-Making: The Group Votes

Instead of one person making the decision, the team often weighs the options together. Let's say you're working on a client presentation. A junior analyst suggests three potential approaches, and the team collectively chooses the best one. This sense of shared ownership is key to how decisions are made.

Information Sharing: Ensuring Everyone Is Informed

When the project is just starting, meetings are essential for sharing crucial information. It's where everyone gets on the same page, ensuring that individual contributions align with broader goals. Information sharing isn't just about talking – it's about alignment.

Feedback: The Path to Improvement

It's common to end meetings with feedback—what went well and what didn't. This culture of continuous improvement helps everyone perform better over time, both individually and as a team.

Accountability: Keeping Everyone on Track

Meetings are where accountability is built. Everyone knows their role, and in the next meeting, there's an expectation to report back. It keeps the project moving, with everyone contributing.

The Power of Self-Reliance in the Workplace

One of the best examples I can share with you comes from my own childhood friend, Joachim. We grew up together, and I've had the privilege of watching him evolve from a curious, adventurous kid into one of the most brilliant lawyers at Wiersholm, one of Norway's top law firms. His journey is one we can all learn from, especially when it comes to how to participate in a meeting.

Joachim's approach in meetings is what sets him apart—not because he's always right, but because he's not afraid to be wrong. He's willing to speak up, even when the stakes are high, and the outcome is uncertain.

I remember him telling me about one particular client meeting, where they were discussing a crucial litigation strategy. The room was filled with senior partners, each one bringing decades of experience to the table. Many people, especially someone in Joachim's position, might have felt intimidated, keeping their ideas to themselves. But not Joachim.

He laid out an idea that was unorthodox and risky. The room fell silent for a moment, the kind of silence that makes you wonder if you've just overstepped. One of the senior partners gave him a skeptical look, the kind that could make anyone rethink their confidence. But Joachim didn't back down. He stood by his analysis, his confidence unwavering. And while the initial reaction was lukewarm, his proposal ignited a conversation. It challenged the team to think differently, and in the end, they came up with a better solution—one that wouldn't have been possible without Joachim's willingness to be bold.

This wasn't a one-off incident. Joachim's reputation was built on moments like this. Not every idea he presented was groundbreaking, but that didn't matter. His partners came to value him because once in a while, he would present something brilliant. Something no one else had thought of. And those moments, the one-in-ten flashes of genius, were enough to justify his higher hourly rate and his growing influence in the firm.

So, what can we take from this? Joachim's story teaches us that in Western workplaces, especially in meetings, you're expected to think independently and contribute actively. It's not enough to just agree with the room. You're there to push ideas forward, to offer alternatives, and to be part of the debate. And yes, sometimes you'll be wrong. But the one time you're right, that one bold idea could change everything.

For you, as an Indian professional working with Western companies, this is key. It's not about knowing all the answers but about showing that you're thinking critically and engaging with the conversation.

In the West, meetings are where recognition is earned. Don't be afraid to speak up, even if it feels risky.

Maximizing Your Impact Through Meeting Preparation

Success in Western meetings doesn't begin when you walk through the door—it starts well before that. Preparation is key to ensuring that when you sit down at the table, you can confidently contribute and make your voice heard. Whether you're given a detailed agenda or just a general topic, preparation allows you to understand the discussion points, anticipate challenges, and offer insightful contributions.

Imagine receiving an agenda for a meeting—this is your roadmap. Instead of simply reviewing it, take some time to think about your position on each topic. Ask yourself questions like:

- *Do I agree with all the proposed deadlines or targets?*
- *Is there a part of the project that needs more focus?*
- *What can I bring to the table that could enhance the team's approach?*

In Western meetings, it's expected that everyone—regardless of rank—comes ready to participate. Simply agreeing with what's already on the table may cause your input to be overlooked. Preparing thoroughly gives you a chance to add value to the conversation and, more importantly, stand out to your peers and superiors.

Let's put this into a practical example. Say you're preparing for a meeting called 'Status on Project'. How should you prepare?

- **Review the Current Project Status**: Take some time to understand the latest updates and prepare a summary of where things stand. Being able to give a concise overview makes you look organized and informed.
- **Identify Key Focus Areas**: Think ahead—where does the team need to concentrate its efforts moving forward? Make recommendations based on your observations. For example, if a particular aspect of the project needs attention, come prepared with suggestions.
- **Anticipate Challenges**: Every project faces hurdles. Instead of waiting for them to arise during the meeting, think ahead about potential roadblocks. Not only will you be ready to address these issues, but you can also come equipped with potential solutions. For example, maybe a deadline seems too tight. If so, suggest realistic adjustments or additional resources that could help.

Western colleagues value this kind of forward-thinking and problem-solving. They appreciate when team members are proactive and take ownership of issues, even before they are fully realized.

By preparing in these ways, you'll be seen as someone who is reliable, thoughtful, and solution-oriented—traits that Western colleagues highly value. Remember, meetings are an opportunity to showcase your critical thinking and communication skills. Simply showing up isn't enough. It's about contributing in a way that helps the team make informed decisions and move forward efficiently.

Ready to Debate?

Imagine this: you're sitting in a meeting, and a bold idea comes up that challenges the status quo. You know you have valid points to

add, but to make an impact, you need more than just good ideas—
you need the ability to debate effectively. The key to success?
Preparation, active listening, and strategic presentation. These are
the building blocks of persuasive arguments in Western meetings,
where decisions are often shaped through debate and discussion.

Debating in meetings isn't about being confrontational. It's
about engaging thoughtfully and constructively with differing
opinions, moving the team toward better decisions. In Western
work environments, presenting your perspective confidently and
respectfully is not just welcomed—it's expected. To navigate
debates successfully, preparation is your first step. Just as a
lawyer prepares thoroughly for a case, you should know your
argument inside and out before stepping into the meeting room.
Take time to:

Before the Meeting

1. Understand Your Argument: Know the core message and
   the data supporting it. Whether you're advocating for a new
   project strategy or offering a critique, make sure you have
   your facts straight and know why your position holds value.
2. Identify Weaknesses: Every argument has its vulnerabilities.
   Acknowledge these beforehand so you aren't caught off
   guard. By being honest with yourself about potential weak
   spots, you can strengthen your position and craft responses
   to inevitable challenges.
3. Anticipate Counterarguments: Put yourself in your
   colleagues' shoes. What objections might they raise? What
   concerns will they have? Preparing rebuttals in advance
   ensures that you can respond thoughtfully when these
   concerns are voiced.

Once the meeting begins, the stage is set, and how you deliver your argument is just as important as what you say. Here's a strategy to ensure you communicate effectively:

During the Meeting

1. Listen Actively: Before jumping in with your ideas, listen carefully to what's being said. This shows respect and allows you to better understand your colleagues' perspectives, which you can then address in your own argument. Listening also allows you to gauge the tone of the meeting—are people being conservative, or is there room for bold ideas?

2. Present Your Argument Clearly: When it's your turn, state your argument concisely and confidently. Begin with your strongest points, capturing attention from the start. For example, *"I'd like to suggest a phased approach to this project, which, while requiring an initial investment, will save us 30% on operational costs within two years."*

3. Address Counterarguments Proactively: Once you've laid out your argument, tackle potential criticisms head-on. This is where your preparation shines. Say something like, *"I understand the concern about upfront costs, but let's consider the long-term benefits that offset these expenses"*. By addressing objections before they are raised, you show foresight and decisiveness.

4. Engage with Respect: Debating in Western meetings isn't about dominating the room. It's about constructive dialogue. Acknowledge valid points made by your colleagues while presenting your own case. For example, if someone raises a valid concern, respond with, *"I see where you're coming from, and that's a fair point. However, I think we can address that by..."*

The goal is to contribute to the conversation without making it about winning or losing—because the best decisions often come from a blend of ideas.

In my own career, I learned the importance of effective debate while working with the partners at one of the 'big four'. My partners, sharp and experienced, never settled for superficial arguments. They demanded depth, rigor, and foresight in every discussion. I quickly realized that if I didn't come to meetings fully prepared—armed with both solid evidence for my ideas and counterarguments for their inevitable critiques—my contributions wouldn't carry weight.

What I have learned is that meetings aren't just about presenting your findings – they're about proving them. You can't just walk in with your data and expect everyone to nod along. You need to anticipate the questions, prepare for pushback, and have the confidence to defend your ideas. Over time, this approach earned me respect. It wasn't just that I was doing the work; it was that I was showing I could think critically about it and handle any challenge threw in my way.

Actively speak up – don't hold back on sharing ideas or addressing problems

Looking back to Arjun and Priya from early in this chapter, they had now understood and learned the dynamics of Western meetings and were ready to navigate this new territory. They understood that Western meetings valued open discussion, direct feedback, and collective decision-making. Armed with this knowledge, they approached their next meeting at GlobalTech with a renewed perspective.

As they entered the conference room, Mark and Susan greeted each other warmly. The agenda was clear: to finalize the design of the new software interface. Unlike before, Arjun and Priya were prepared to engage in a more interactive and spontaneous discussion.

MARK: Welcome, everyone. Let's dive into the design of the user dashboard. We need to decide on the layout and the key features we want to include. Susan, would you like to start with your thoughts?

SUSAN: Sure. I think we should focus on making the dashboard intuitive and user-friendly. What if we incorporate a customizable widget area for users to personalize their experience?

Priya nodded, feeling more comfortable voicing her opinion directly in the meeting.

PRIYA: That's an excellent idea, Susan. I believe adding customizable widgets will greatly enhance user engagement. However, we need to ensure that the customization options do not overwhelm the users. Perhaps we could limit the number of widgets they can add?

Mark noticed the shift in Priya's approach and appreciated her direct involvement.

MARK: Great point, Priya. Limiting the widgets is a good idea. Arjun, what are your thoughts on this?

Arjun, recalling the importance of real-time collaboration, shared his insights without hesitation.

ARJUN: I agree with both of you. Customizable widgets are a valuable addition. We should also consider including a help section or tutorials within the dashboard to guide users on how to customize their interface effectively.

Susan smiled, acknowledging Arjun's valuable input.

SUSAN: That's a fantastic suggestion, Arjun. Including tutorials will certainly help users make the most of the customization features.

The discussion flowed smoothly, with everyone contributing their ideas openly. There was a palpable sense of collaboration in the room. They moved on to the next agenda item: addressing the project timeline.

MARK: We're slightly behind schedule. How can we catch up and ensure we meet our deadlines?

This time, Priya felt confident discussing potential delays and seeking immediate solutions.

PRIYA: We've identified a few bottlenecks in the development phase. To catch up, we need to allocate additional resources or adjust some of our milestones. Arjun and I have already discussed this with our team, and we have a few suggestions.

Mark appreciated the proactive approach.

MARK: Excellent, Priya. Let's hear your suggestions.

Arjun presented his plan, which included reallocating tasks and extending work hours for critical milestones. The team discussed and refined the plan collectively, ensuring everyone was on board.

By the end of the meeting, they had not only finalized the design but also developed a concrete plan to get the project back on track. The room buzzed with a sense of accomplishment and mutual respect.

As they wrapped up, Mark turned to Arjun and Priya.

MARK: I'm impressed with how you both engaged today. Your contributions were invaluable. This is exactly how we can achieve the best results together.

Arjun and Priya exchanged a satisfied glance, knowing they had successfully adapted to the Western meeting style. They left the room confident in their ability to navigate future meetings with the same effectiveness, bridging cultural gaps and fostering a truly collaborative work environment.

Navigating the dynamics of Western meetings can be a transformative experience for professionals from diverse cultural backgrounds. For Indian professionals, understanding and mastering the nuances of Western meeting practices can significantly enhance their effectiveness and integration into global teams. This chapter has explored several key aspects, including the importance of preparation, the value of self-reliance and individualism, and the art of debating. Together, these elements form a comprehensive guide to thriving in Western meetings.

- **Preparation** is the foundation of success in any meeting. As we discussed, knowing the agenda or the general purpose of the meeting allows you to prepare your thoughts and contributions effectively. By anticipating the topics of discussion, identifying your stance, and understanding potential challenges, you can enter meetings with confidence and clarity. This proactive approach not only demonstrates your commitment and professionalism but also ensures that you can contribute meaningfully to the discussion.

- Western meetings often value **self-reliance and individualism,** encouraging participants to trust in their abilities and take initiative. By preparing thoroughly, considering both the strengths and weaknesses of your arguments, and being willing to present and defend your ideas, you embody these values. Remember, it's not about being right all the time but about contributing thoughtfully and learning from the process.

- **Debating** is an integral part of Western meetings, where the free exchange of ideas and critical thinking are highly prized. Effective debating involves not only presenting your arguments clearly but also anticipating and addressing counterarguments. By listening actively, engaging respectfully, and presenting well-prepared points, you can navigate debates successfully.

The skills discussed in this chapter are not just about fitting into a Western framework but about bringing your unique strengths to the table and enriching the collaborative process. As you continue to grow and adapt, remember that the ultimate goal is to contribute to a productive, inclusive, and innovative meeting environment. Now you're ready for your next meeting - just remember to lower your shoulders, speak your mind and bear in mind that your Western colleagues or clients are eager to hear your thoughts.

In the next chapter, we'll dive into the final skill: how to present yourself. Think of this skill as the glue that holds everything else together. Without it, even the strongest skills can falter, overshadowed by distractions that drown out what you truly want to communicate. Let's step into the final section of the book and bring it all together.

Skill 8: *Become comfortable with expressing your opinions, making independent choices, and participating actively in discussions during* **meetings** *to reach a decision. The purpose of a meeting is to discuss and agree on decisions together.*

Advice for Indians:

1. It's harder to offend Westerners than Indians, so don't worry about disagreeing with them, critiquing something they say, or offering a different opinion—they expect this.
2. Avoid agreeing with something during a meeting and then calling the Westerner later to disagree; try to express your disagreement during the meeting itself.
3. If you don't understand something a Westerner has explained, ask for clarification in the meeting (not later in a phone call or email).
4. If a Westerner uses idioms or expressions you don't understand, ask for their meanings during the meeting.
5. There's no need for frequent breaks; address issues directly during the meeting.
6. Accept critique or negative feedback during the meeting and focus on understanding the reasons behind it.
7. Always prepare for meetings. If there's an agenda, write down points and be ready to discuss them. If there's no agenda, create one, send it out to the team, and prepare for each point to ensure you're ready for discussion.

Exercise: Effective Meeting Preparation and Participation

Objective: Prepare a discussion-focused agenda to make your meetings productive and collaborative.

1. **Create an Agenda with Discussion Points**: Before your next meeting, outline key topics as discussion points, not just updates. For each item, include a question or decision point to encourage team input and engagement.

2. **Send the Agenda in Advance**: Email the agenda to the team at least one day before the meeting. This gives everyone time to think about each topic and come prepared to discuss.

3. **Lead and Participate Actively**: During the meeting, introduce each discussion point, share your input briefly, then invite the team to contribute. This shifts the focus from simply informing to collaborative problem-solving.

4. **Follow Up if Needed**: After the meeting, send a quick summary of decisions made and any action items to keep everyone aligned and accountable.

9

The Professional Edge: How to Present Yourself with Confidence

❧✳❧

Elevating your professionalism through attire, improving virtual presence, and confidence

Elevate Your Presence, Elevate Your Success

Rajesh had been preparing for this meeting all week. As an IT consultant from India, he was excited to discuss his innovative ideas with Simon, a potential client from the U.K. Simon, a seasoned professional, was eager to hear how Rajesh could help streamline his company's IT processes.

The meeting started promptly, but things quickly began to unravel. Rajesh's Wi-Fi, which had been acting up all morning, decided to betray him at the worst possible moment. His voice crackled, and the video feed lagged, creating an awkward start to the conversation. As he spoke passionately about his proposals, Simon struggled to piece together what was being said.

Adding to the challenge, Rajesh's webcam was positioned at an odd angle, capturing mostly the ceiling and casting his face in shadow. The video quality was poor, pixelating his expressions and further distancing him from the conversation. He had opted for a casual t-shirt instead of a more formal outfit, thinking the focus should be on his ideas, not his appearance. But Simon, used to a more polished presentation, found the informality jarring.

The backdrop of Rajesh's home office was equally distracting. A cluttered bookshelf and an open door revealing family members walking by intermittently stole Simon's attention. Midway through Rajesh's explanation, a loud burst of laughter erupted from the next room, forcing Rajesh to apologize and try to regain his train of thought.

Despite the technical glitches and chaotic environment, Rajesh was confident in his pitch. He spoke quickly, eager to cover all the points he had meticulously prepared. But to Simon, who was accustomed to a more measured pace and clear communication, it was overwhelming. He strained to keep up with Rajesh's rapid speech, feeling increasingly frustrated.

By the time the meeting ended, Simon was left with a headache and little understanding of what Rajesh had tried to convey. The ideas, though brilliant, were lost in a sea of poor presentation and distractions. Simon sighed, feeling that the entire meeting had been a waste of time. Rajesh, unaware of the impact his setup had made, was puzzled by the lack of enthusiasm from Simon.

The potential collaboration faded, not because Rajesh lacked expertise, but because the wrapping – the presentation – had overshadowed the content.

The story you just read is inspired by true events—situations I have witnessed firsthand or heard about from colleagues and clients over the years. While the story may be slightly exaggerated, with everything that could go wrong indeed going wrong, it highlights a scenario that plays out far too often when professionals from India engage with their counterparts in the West. The potential for success is there, but small, easily avoidable mistakes can derail even the most promising of meetings.

Luckily, these issues are among the easiest to fix. With a few quick adjustments, the problems that plagued Rajesh's meeting—bad Wi-Fi, fast-paced speaking, distracting backgrounds—can be entirely avoided. However, as we delve deeper into this chapter, you'll uncover powerful strategies that go beyond fixing these surface-level issues. This chapter may not initially seem like the most important, **but it is the glue that holds everything together**. If this doesn't sit right, all the other chapters might become meaningless. After completing this chapter, you should be able to: *Recognize the importance of professionalism by focusing on formal attire, improving your virtual presence, and communicating with confidence and clarity.*

Birds of a Feather Flock Together

Where do you think the slogan "Birds of a feather flock together" comes from? In Norway, we have a similar saying: "Like barn leker best," which directly translates to "Similar children play best." It's a phrase that captures a universal truth—the idea that people naturally gravitate toward others who are like them.

These sayings, across cultures, highlight a key principle: people are naturally attracted to those who share similarities with them. In international business, especially when working with Western clients or colleagues, this concept takes on crucial significance. Success in these settings often hinges not just on your technical skills or knowledge but on your ability to align with the cultural expectations and norms of your counterparts.

The Indian concept of "जहां की मिट्टी, वहां का रंग" embodies the idea of finding and asserting one's place within a group by adapting to its norms and expectations. This principle is particularly relevant when considering how to present oneself in different professional environments. Just as individuals are naturally drawn to those who seem similar, it's often necessary to adjust one's appearance and communication style to align with the professional standards of a given setting.

This adaptation isn't about losing individuality; rather, it's about recognizing that to be accepted and successful within a particular 'gang' or professional community, one must fit in visually and behaviorally. For instance, in a professional setting, this might mean wearing formal attire, demonstrating confidence, and communicating clearly. These adjustments help you blend in with your peers and establish your place within the group.

Presenting Yourself Professionally

When it comes to professional success, how you present yourself can be just as important as the ideas you bring to the table. It's important to remember that while everyone is different—and those differences are valuable—sometimes standing out too much, like wearing a bright yellow shirt in a sea of blue suits, can draw the wrong kind of attention. The key is to find a balance between maintaining your individuality and fitting into the professional environment. For example, I personally like to wear bracelets as a small expression of my own style, but when it comes to the overall attire, I stick to the standard blue formal suits, just like everyone else in my industry.

One crucial lesson I learned during my time as a consultant was the importance of mirroring your clients' dress code. The rule was simple: if your clients wore suits, you wore a suit. If they opted for blazers, you did the same. And if they dressed semi-formally, so did you. But the overall rule is to be overdressed rather than underdressed. This practice wasn't just about blending in; it was about showing respect and building rapport by demonstrating that you understood and valued their professional culture.

Dress Codes in Different Industries

Reflection point: Take a moment to reflect on the dress culture among your friends. Is there a particular style that stands out? Now, consider the dress code at your workplace – do you notice any differences?

In the west, same as in India, dress codes vary widely across industries, each with its own unspoken rules and standards. In the financial world, for instance, the dress code is almost uniform—think dark suits, crisp white shirts, and polished shoes. The 'Patagonia vest' has even become something of a symbol. When I started in finance, I made it a point to buy five blue suits. Why? Because adopting the expected dress code helped me fit in and be taken seriously. It's about blending in with the crowd so that your ideas, rather than your attire, stand out.

On the other hand, tech companies have their own distinct style. While it may be more casual—think jeans, t-shirts, and hoodies—the uniformity is still there. Everyone dresses similarly, creating an unspoken sense of belonging. Even in this casual environment, following the dress code is important because it shows you understand and respect the culture.

The Importance of Adapting

Adopting the appropriate dress code is not about losing your individuality but about recognizing the impact of visual cues in professional settings. For example, there are stories of people who faced criticism for wearing shorts in an office environment where such attire was deemed inappropriate and negatively affected the overall impression of that individual.

It's important to understand that dress codes are more than just a formality – they help create a sense of unity and professionalism. When you dress in a way that aligns with the expectations of your industry, you create the illusion that the differences between you and your colleagues or clients are smaller than they actually are. This can make interactions smoother and help you integrate more seamlessly into the professional environment.

In many cases, dressing appropriately is not an icebreaker but rather a simple change that can vastly improve how you are perceived. By adopting the right attire, you send a message that you understand the industry's culture and are serious about being a part of it. This small adjustment can enhance your overall professional image, making you appear more competent, confident, and aligned with the norms of the industry you are working in.

Roadmap for Understanding Dress Codes in Various Industries: Western Clients

This roadmap will guide you in understanding the dress codes of different industries when interacting with Western clients. Dress codes can vary significantly depending on the industry, company culture, and location, so it's crucial to adapt to each situation accordingly. And remember the below are just general guidelines, a first and top-down view of the attire in the specific industries. When you join a firm, it's important to start by following the dress code outlined below. Once you're settled, you can assess and adapt your attire as needed to align with the company's culture and expectations.

1. Corporate/Finance Industry (Banking, Finance, Investment, Law)
   - **Dress Code: Business Formal**
   - **Key Elements:**
     - **Men:** Dark-colored suits (black, navy, or gray), white or light-colored dress shirts (white or light blue), conservative ties, polished dress shoes.
     - **Women:** Tailored suits (pantsuits or skirt suits), conservative blouses, closed-toe heels, minimal jewelry.
   - **Tips:** Avoid flashy colors or patterns. Maintain a polished and professional appearance.

2. Technology Industry (IT, Software Development, Startups)
   - **Dress Code: Business Casual**
   - **Key Elements:**
     - **Men:** Dress shirts or polo shirts, chinos or slacks, loafers or dress shoes. Jackets are optional.
     - **Women:** Blouses or smart tops, slacks or skirts, flats or low heels. Dresses in conservative styles are also appropriate.
   - **Tips:** The tech industry often values comfort and practicality, but it's important to maintain a neat and tidy appearance. Avoid overly casual items like graphic t-shirts or athletic wear unless you're sure of the company's culture. If you're an IT consultant, the business attire is often more formal compared to employees working directly within the organization, so keep this in mind.

3. Creative Industries (Advertising, Media, Fashion, Design)
   - **Dress Code: Creative Casual**

- **Key Elements:**
  - **Men:** Stylish but relaxed attire, such as well-fitted jeans or chinos, smart casual shirts, blazers, or casual jackets. Sneakers or stylish shoes.
  - **Women:** Fashion-forward outfits, including trendy dresses, skirts, or tailored pants, paired with stylish tops. Fashionable shoes.

- **Tips:** Express individuality while maintaining professionalism. Bold colors, patterns, and accessories are often welcomed, but always ensure the outfit is appropriate for the work environment.

General Tips:

- **Research the Company Culture:** Before meetings, research the company's dress code through their website, social media, or by asking contacts.
- **When in Doubt, Overdress:** It's better to be slightly overdressed than underdressed in professional settings. A safe choice would always be a white or light blue shirt and blue chinos or suit trousers.
- **Consider the Occasion:** Adjust your attire depending on whether the occasion is a regular workday, a client meeting, or a formal event.

It's always better to err on the side of formality rather than risk being too casual. A plain-colored shirt, preferably light blue or white, is often the safest choice. Remember, your clothes should not be the focus—your professionalism and competence should be.

Indian culture embraces vibrant colors and diverse attire, but when working with Western clients, it's wise to start with a more formal approach. As you get to know your client's preferences, you can adjust accordingly. If your client frequently wears t-shirts, you may consider dressing down slightly, but never to the point of looking sloppy.

Always maintain a neat appearance: keep your hair well-groomed, shave or trim your beard, and ensure your overall look is polished. Your appearance speaks volumes about your professionalism.

Improving Your Virtual Presence

In today's globalized work environment, where virtual meetings and online collaborations have become the norm, your virtual presence plays a crucial role in how you are perceived by your colleagues, clients, and partners. As a professional, it's essential to ensure that your virtual presence meets, if not exceeds, the expectations of those you interact with. Remember your virtual presence is not just about being visible on the screen; it's about how you present yourself, how clearly you communicate, and how professional you appear. In a virtual setting, where physical cues are limited, these elements become even more significant. A subpar virtual presence can negatively affect the quality of your interactions, leading to misunderstandings, reduced credibility, and missed opportunities. Conversely, a polished and professional virtual presence can enhance your reputation, foster trust, and facilitate smoother communication.

Webcam

One of the simplest yet most effective ways to improve your virtual presence is by investing in high-quality equipment. This may seem like a no-brainer, but it is surprising how often this aspect is overlooked. In Norway's consultancy world, for example, having the right equipment is considered standard practice, and anything less is viewed as unprofessional.

- **HD Camera:** The first step is to invest in a good HD camera for your PC. A high-definition camera ensures that you appear clear and sharp on screen. This not only makes you look more professional but also allows others to read your facial expressions and body language more accurately, which is essential for effective communication.

- **Quality Microphone:** Next, invest in a good quality microphone. Clear audio is just as important as a clear image. A poor microphone can result in muffled sound or background noise, which can be distracting, unprofessional, but more importantly, your ideas might not be heard. A good microphone ensures that your voice is heard clearly, making your communication more effective.

Lighting and Camera Positioning

Proper lighting and camera positioning are critical factors in creating a professional virtual presence. Ensure that your face is well-lit by using natural light or an appropriate desk lamp. Avoid having bright light sources directly behind you, as they can cause glare or make you appear as a silhouette. The camera should be at eye level, not too high or too low, to avoid the unflattering 'up-the-nose' angle or the downward gaze that can make you appear disengaged.

Body Language and Posture

Just as in a physical meeting, your body language speaks volumes in a virtual setting. Sit up straight, avoid fidgeting, and maintain a calm and composed demeanor. These subtle cues can convey confidence and professionalism, reinforcing your verbal communication. Even in a virtual environment, how you carry yourself impacts how others perceive your competence and confidence.

Ensuring Stable Connectivity

Having a stable Wi-Fi connection is non-negotiable. Dropped connections or poor-quality video due to unstable internet can disrupt the flow of the meeting and make you appear unprepared.

Make sure your Wi-Fi is strong and reliable, especially if you're working from home. If necessary, invest in a better router or use a wired connection to ensure stability.

Managing Background Noise

Background noise can be a major distraction during virtual meetings. If you're working from home, make sure that no one interrupts you or speaks in the background. Inform your family members or roommates about your meeting schedule to avoid disruptions. If you work in an open office environment, find a quiet room where you can conduct your meetings without interruptions.

Creating a Professional Background

Your background should be professional and free from distractions. In today's world, many platforms allow you to blur your background or use a virtual background with your company's logo. If you're at home, use this feature to maintain a clean, distraction-free environment. If you're in the office, ensure that your background is simple, ideally a plain wall, with no distracting elements like moving objects or clutter.

Testing and Preparation

Before any important meeting, take a few minutes to test your equipment and ensure everything is working correctly. This includes checking your camera, microphone, and internet connection. Also, prepare for the meeting as you would for an in-person one—review the agenda, know your talking points, and be ready to engage actively. This preparation shows respect for others' time and demonstrates your commitment to the discussion.

Remember, improving your virtual presence is not just about following a checklist; it's about understanding that every detail contributes to the overall impression you make on your colleagues and clients. By investing in the right equipment, ensuring proper lighting and camera positioning, maintaining professional body language, preparing thoroughly, ensuring stable connectivity, and creating a distraction-free environment, you can enhance your virtual presence. This, in turn, will help you build better relationships, communicate more effectively, and succeed in your interactions with Western professionals. In a world where first impressions often happen through a screen, making these improvements is not just advisable—it's essential.

Communicate With Confidence and Clarity

In professional settings, especially when working with Western counterparts, communication goes beyond just sharing facts – it's about how you deliver your message. Confidence and clarity are the keys to making a lasting impact. For Indian professionals, enhancing these two skills can greatly improve how your ideas are perceived and respected. It's not just about being heard; it's about making sure your message is taken seriously and acted upon.

This idea of shaping perception ties perfectly with the story of Petter Stordalen, the renowned Norwegian entrepreneur. While managing City Syd shopping center in Trondheim, Stordalen filled the parking lot with rental cars to create the illusion of a thriving business, even though customer traffic was still low. This clever tactic gave people the impression of success before it had fully arrived.

Like Stordalen, we can control how others perceive us in professional settings. In virtual meetings especially, it's not just what you say that matters—it's how you present your message. Just as Stordalen's clever display of 'success' helped build the image of a bustling center, how you communicate and dress can shape how your audience views you and your ideas. By speaking clearly, pacing your words thoughtfully, perfect lighting, clothes, web-cap, sound, and focusing on what matters to your audience, you ensure your message is delivered with the impact you intend. It's about creating the right perception, much like how Stordalen's audience believed in the success of the shopping center before it truly happened.

Confidence: The Power of Self-Assurance

Confidence is about more than just speaking; it's about how you present yourself. When you speak with confidence, you demonstrate that you believe in your message and your ability to contribute meaningfully to the discussion. This is especially important in virtual meetings where physical presence is limited, and your voice and demeanor become your primary tools for making an impact.

Communicating Clearly: Techniques for Effective Speech

Clear communication is essential for ensuring that your message is understood as intended. Too often, the speed and manner of speaking can hinder this process, particularly when your audience is not accustomed to your accent or speaking style. Here are some techniques to help you communicate with clarity:

Slow Down

One of the more common challenges that Indian professionals face is the tendency to speak too quickly. While this may be natural when conversing with other Indians, it can be a barrier when communicating with foreigners. I've heard countless times from my colleagues in Europe and the U.S that they struggle to keep up with the pace at which some of their Indian counterparts speak, resulting in misunderstandings.

I have received feedback from my Western colleagues highlighting a key aspect of communication: it's not just about what you say but how you say it. In many Indian contexts, speed is often mistaken for efficiency. Mistakenly assuming that speaking quickly shows confidence and thorough preparation. But in cross-cultural settings, pacing is essential. Slower, more deliberate speech gives your listeners time to process and engage with your ideas. Remember that effective communication isn't about filling every second with information—it's about creating space for understanding. Even if you're confident in your language skills, the way you deliver your thoughts matters just as much. Slow down. Let your words sink in.

The lesson here is clear: when you think you are speaking slowly enough, speak even slower. This may feel painfully slow to you, but for your international audience, it will likely be just right.

Eye Contact and Direct Engagement

When speaking in a virtual meeting, it's crucial to look directly into the camera. This mimics eye contact, helping to create a connection with your audience. When you look at the camera, it feels as though you are speaking directly to the person, making your communication more personal and engaging.

Use Pauses Effectively

Pausing at key points in your speech not only allows your audience to absorb what you've said but also gives you time to gather your thoughts. Strategic pauses can emphasize important points, making your message more impactful.

The Importance of Pronunciation and Accent

Language proficiency is a key asset for Indian professionals, but accent and pronunciation can sometimes pose challenges in international settings. Every country has its own dialect, and the way your native language influences your English can impact how you are perceived. In Norway, for example, there is a noticeable difference between those who work regularly in international contexts and those who do not. The more you practice English, particularly with native speakers from the U.K. or the U.S., the less your native accent will overshadow your speech.

The goal here is not to completely eliminate your accent – that's neither necessary nor desirable. Instead, it's about refining your pronunciation to the point where your speech is easily understood by an international audience. When your English is clear enough that someone from the U.K. or America doesn't immediately recognize that it's not your first language, you've truly succeeded. This level of clarity not only enhances communication but also boosts your credibility and professionalism.

The glue that holds everything together

Looking back on the story of Rajesh, he reflected on a disappointing meeting with Simon. He took a step back to reflect on what had gone wrong. He realized that while his ideas were strong, the way he presented them had fallen short. Determined to improve, Rajesh spent the next few weeks learning and refining his approach.

Now, with another opportunity to impress Simon, Rajesh was ready to put his new knowledge to the test.

The meeting started promptly, just as before, but this time everything was different. Rajesh had upgraded his Wi-Fi to ensure a stable connection, and as soon as the call began, the video feed was sharp and smooth. Simon noticed the immediate improvement and felt more at ease.

Rajesh had also taken the time to perfect his setup. His webcam was now positioned at eye level, capturing him from the best angle. His face was well-lit, with soft lighting that highlighted his expressions without casting any distracting shadows. Rajesh had chosen a crisp, white shirt for the meeting, paired with a subtle tie, projecting a professional image that Simon instantly respected.

The background of Rajesh's home office was a model of simplicity and professionalism – a neat bookshelf and a closed door provided a distraction-free environment. There were no interruptions this time; Rajesh had ensured that his surroundings were quiet, with no background noise to break his focus or Simon's attention.

When Rajesh began to speak, his voice was clear and confident, the result of days spent practicing his delivery. He had learned to pace himself, speaking at a measured rhythm that allowed Simon to follow along easily. Rajesh had also prepared visual aids that he shared seamlessly during the presentation, helping to illustrate his points and keep Simon engaged.

By the end of the meeting, Simon was impressed not only by the content of Rajesh's proposals but also by the polished and confident manner in which they were delivered. The contrast to their previous encounter was striking, and Simon could see the effort Rajesh had put into refining his presentation.

Rajesh's journey teaches us a valuable lesson about the importance of going the extra mile. Success isn't just about having great ideas; it's about how you present those ideas to others. By making simple but effective changes—like improving his internet connection, refining his appearance, and organizing his environment—Rajesh transformed a potential failure into a success.

Recognizing the importance of professionalism means focusing on formal attire, enhancing your virtual presence, and communicating with confidence and clarity. These elements are crucial in ensuring that your ideas are not only heard but also respected and acted upon.

Setting yourself up for success requires taking full control of your presentation, leaving nothing to chance. These seemingly minor adjustments can significantly impact how you are perceived and whether your ideas resonate. When you take ownership of every aspect of your setup and delivery, you're not just sharing your ideas—you're making sure they shine. In the end, it's the combination of great ideas and polished presentation that paves the way for meaningful success.

Skill 9: Recognize the importance of professionalism by focusing on formal attire, improving your virtual presence, and communicating with confidence and clarity.

Action Points Going Forward

1. **Dress Code and Appearance:** Study the clothing of your peers in the West and adopt a similar style. Choose attire that aligns with professional standards. Ensure your overall appearance is polished, including well-groomed hair and a clean shave.

2. **Upgrade Your Tech Setup:** Invest in a high-definition webcam, a quality microphone, and ensure consistent internet connectivity. Position your camera at eye level for a more engaging connection and pay attention to lighting to make sure your face is well-lit.

3. **Prepare Your Environment:** Organize your workspace to be free of distractions, with a tidy and professional background. Ensure your environment is quiet, with no background noise.

4. **Effective Communication:** Practice speaking slowly and clearly, slowly adapting to a U.K. or American accent if necessary. Engage in active listening by responding thoughtfully, sharing your views and opinions confidently.

Epilogue

Putting the Skills to work

❧✳❧

A Tribute to India

This book is my tribute to India—the country I have grown to admire and cherish in all its richness. When I first learned I would be sent to India, I knew my life would change in ways I couldn't yet predict. The moment I arrived, I was swept up in an experience so vivid that it left a lasting imprint on me. The streets buzzed with a symphony of sounds—honking cars, vibrant conversations, and the rhythmic chants of street vendors—all merging into a chaotic harmony that was uniquely Indian.

The crowds moved like a river, each person carrying their own story, each encounter a reminder of the vast diversity and shared humanity that binds us. The heat was an ever-present force, wrapping around me like a familiar embrace, bringing out the vibrancy in everything I saw—the radiant saris, the rich aroma of spices, the lush landscapes glowing under the golden light of the sun. Yet, it was the people who left the greatest impression—their warmth, their generosity, and their openness made me feel welcome in a land that was foreign, yet somehow felt like home.

And then there was the food. Each dish was a story in itself—a burst of flavors that took me deeper into the heart of

Indian culture. The spices told tales of history, tradition, and the land they came from, each bite revealing something new. India's history wasn't just found in monuments or temples; it lived in the streets, in the stories people shared, and in the everyday life that unfolded around me.

When I first arrived on assignment in India, the task seemed straightforward: deliver courses on financial due diligence. I came prepared with knowledge and purpose, believing I was there to teach. But it didn't take long for me to realize that the team in India was not in need of instruction on the technicalities – they had mastered those long before I arrived. The issue wasn't about skills; it was far more nuanced.

We had long assumed that the difficulties in working with our Indian colleagues stemmed from a lack of education or experience. How wrong we were. The truth was that we weren't struggling with competence – we were struggling with culture. The barriers we faced weren't due to a lack of knowledge but rather a gap in understanding – different expectations, unspoken norms, and the subtleties of communication that come from years of ingrained cultural habits.

Over the seven years leading up to my time in India, we had unknowingly stumbled through these cultural divides, misattributing our setbacks to the wrong causes. We missed the real issue: it wasn't that the team didn't know how to do the work; it was that we didn't know how to work with them in a way that respected and understood their approach.

The misunderstandings, frustrations, and missteps were not signs of incompetence. They were simply the results of failing to bridge the cultural gap.

To my team in India, my former colleagues, and every Indian professional aspiring to thrive in a global workforce, this book is for you. Although it comes later than it should, my hope is that it will still make a lasting difference. These nine skills are what I wish I had shared with you from the beginning—not just to help you master technical skills but to guide you in navigating the cultural bridges between East and West. They represent what I've learned—often through trial and error—about how you can succeed when working with the West. These skills form a roadmap for building stronger relationships, avoiding common pitfalls, and creating success in any global context.

What You've Learned:

You now have the tools to succeed—not just to survive, but to thrive. Let's recap the key skills you've learned:

1. **Understand Why You Need to Adapt to Western Culture**
   Adapting isn't about losing who you are; it's about growing. The ability to bridge cultures is your greatest asset. The Western workplace operates with a different set of rules and expectations. By understanding the **need to adapt**, you'll avoid the misunderstandings that could otherwise lead to failed relationships and missed opportunities. Adaptation means recognizing that you can still honor your own culture while **enhancing your professional capabilities.**

2. **Embrace Fast-Paced Relationship-Building**
   Skip formalities and interact with new colleagues as if you've known them for years. Take the initiative instead of waiting for invitations. Break initial barriers with casual small talk, light-hearted humor, and conversations about

shared interests or social activities. Once the connection is made, nurture the relationship naturally, just as you would back home. Relationships in the West matter, but they move faster and carry less weight in business than in India. Focus 20% on relationships and 80% on delivering value for your client, employer, or business partner.

3. **Master Clear, Honest Communication**

   In the West, **direct communication** is valued. Be clear, be honest, and don't worry about being perceived as rude. What may feel blunt to you is simply efficient communication in the West. Avoid indirect messages or relying on non-verbal cues. The key is to let your words carry the meaning – they are your most important tool. Being **straightforward** reduces misunderstandings and ensures your message is received as intended.

4. **Value Time as a Precious Resource**

   Time is viewed as a **finite resource** in the West. Efficiency, punctuality, and goal-oriented actions are essential. In Western culture, every minute counts, and wasting time can be perceived as disrespectful. **Respect deadlines,** structure your day effectively, and always be punctual. By aligning yourself with this mindset, you'll be seen as dependable and professional—traits that are highly valued in any workplace.

5. **Build Trust Through Consistency**

   Trust is not built through friendships alone, but through **reliability**. In Western workplaces, trust is earned by consistently delivering high-quality work and meeting expectations. It's about showing that you can be counted on, not just once, but **time and again**. When you demonstrate that your work is dependable, you create a foundation of trust that will serve you in every professional relationship.

6. **Convince with Clear, Solution-Focused Arguments**

   In Western professional environments, persuasion is about understanding your counterparts' problems and addressing them with solutions. Be concise and solution-oriented when you present your ideas. Time is precious, so focus on efficiency—get to the point quickly and clearly. Present your arguments with clarity, always keeping the solution in mind. This shows that you're not only aware of the problem, but you're **ready to solve it.**

7. **Engage Directly with Superiors**

   In the West, hierarchy doesn't limit your voice. Open communication is valued at all levels, and your superiors expect you to engage with them directly and take the initiative to identify your own tasks. Don't wait to be managed or handed instructions. Don't hold back—share your ideas and concerns. **Challenge upwards.** Pleasing your superiors without voicing your own thoughts won't lead to progress. Speak up, offer solutions, and prove that you are a valuable **resource,** not just a follower.

8. **Actively Participate in Discussions**

   Meetings are for **decision-making,** and your contribution is essential. Don't hold back in discussions—your input can shape the direction of the team. Be transparent, share your thoughts openly, and don't worry about being perfect. Active participation is key to success in Western workplaces, where collaboration and collective input are highly valued. **Your voice matters.**

9. **Present Yourself Professionally**

   Your professional image is built not just on what you do, but how you present yourself. Whether in-person or virtually, your attire, communication style, and virtual presence matter. Dress the part, speak with confidence, and ensure your online setup—camera, microphone, background—reflects professionalism. **Presentation is the glue** that holds everything together. Without it, even the best work can fall apart.

This book and the skillset presented here are not critiques of Indian culture, nor are they attempts to diminish its value. On the contrary, they are born from a place of deep respect and admiration for the richness and diversity of Indian traditions. **Our cultures,** though vibrant in their own right, have their own nuances, and these **differences can sometimes lead to misunderstandings** that can impede success when working with the West. This book is designed for those who want to bridge that gap, for those who see the value in **adapting and learning** as essential steps toward thriving in a globalized world.

The focus of this journey has been on those **critical moments** where our cultures diverge, and where things can go wrong—not because they always do, but because understanding these moments is the key to overcoming them. It's in these challenges that this book becomes your **roadmap,** guiding you through **unfamiliar territory** with confidence and clarity.

Embrace Your Strengths

Through this process, never forget to embrace your inherent strengths. Your **technical expertise, strong work ethic, quick**

learning ability, respectfulness, and **loyalty** are the qualities that have brought you far. They are the same qualities that will carry you forward. The goal of this book has been to help you **enhance** these attributes by combining them with the **cultural fluency** needed to work successfully with the West.

By incorporating the steps we've discussed—whether it's **adapting to communication styles,** learning to be direct, or understanding the Western perspective on **time and trust**—you place yourself in a position to succeed not just technically but **professionally** in a way that transcends borders.

Change Takes Time

Change is a process, and it doesn't happen overnight. Some cultural shifts will come easily to you—like using first names instead of formal titles—while others, like giving candid feedback or being more spontaneous in meetings, may take time. But each small step is a **valuable part of the journey.** Change begins with a belief in the **value of this knowledge** and a willingness to start small.

Don't expect to master these skills immediately. **Be patient with yourself.** Cultural learning is not a sprint, but a marathon. Each time you consciously **apply these principles** in your work, you'll get a little closer to mastering them.

Be Open and Curious

As you move forward, **stay curious** and **open-minded** about cultural differences. It's okay to acknowledge when things feel unfamiliar or challenging. In fact, being **open** about these differences with your Western colleagues will help **foster understanding.** Don't be afraid to start conversations about how work styles differ—it's through these discussions that real growth happens, both for you and for your team.

Take the first step with confidence, knowing that each effort you make will compound over time. The small changes you implement today will set the foundation for long-term success in your global career.

My First Teach: Rohan's Journey

When I first met Rohan, I saw a bright future ahead of him. He was a young, sharp certified accountant, always energetic, with a professional demeanor that matched his well-groomed appearance. But as talented as he was, I quickly realized that for him to truly succeed in a Western business environment, he needed more than just technical skills. He had to master the subtle cultural nuances that could make or break his success. Our learning wasn't formal—it happened organically through our work together. In project meetings, casual conversations over coffee, or moments between tasks, I would share lessons that weren't found in textbooks. These everyday interactions helped shape Rohan's professional approach, guiding him toward the skills that would later become the foundation of this book.

Building Relationships Through Casual Small Talk

Rohan was naturally joyful and outgoing, always lighting up the office with his banter and jokes among his Indian colleagues. However, I noticed that when he interacted with his Western peers or senior colleagues, his playful side disappeared. He became more serious and reserved, unsure of how to balance professionalism with his natural friendliness. One day, during a coffee break, I told him: "You don't need to change who you are." In fact, in Western offices, building connections beyond work is important. Whether you're talking to a peer, a senior leader, or someone you just met, don't hesitate to share some casual small talk. Talk about the weather, find common interests, discuss recent news, that is how bonds are initially established.

Rohan took the advice to heart and began to engage in light conversations, especially about his favorite hobby—swimming. Whether chatting about his weekend swim or making small talk before meetings, he started to see the difference. His Western colleagues became more open around him, and he built deeper connections, not just within his team but across all levels of seniority. I often heard stories of colleagues that had interacted with him and in contrast to past experiences where my colleagues preferred to work with colleagues in Norway, they now were indifferent to working with Rohan or them. Small **talk wasn't a distraction—it was the foundation for creating stronger professional bonds.**

Building Trust Through Consistency

Delivering high-quality work every time is essential, but there's another side to building trust—**transparency when things go wrong.** Rohan was always committed to doing his best, but there were times when he didn't fully understand certain tasks or made small mistakes. Like many, he was hesitant to admit when something went wrong or when he didn't have all the answers.

One day, we discussed this during a project review. I told him, "In Western workplaces, admitting when you've made a mistake or asking for help is seen as a strength, not a weakness. The worst thing you can do is deliver subpar work without addressing the issues upfront."

From that point forward, Rohan made it a priority to be open about his limitations and raise concerns early. He started asking for help when needed and being transparent about what he didn't understand. This honesty didn't damage his reputation—in fact, it **strengthened** it. His colleagues respected him more for being upfront, and this built a deeper layer of trust between him and his team.

Engaging Directly with Superiors

Rohan was used to deferring to senior leaders and staying quiet during meetings. But in the Western workplace, **open communication with superiors** is not only welcomed, it's expected.

During a project review, I encouraged him to voice his concerns directly to his superior. He hesitated, unsure of how it would be received. "Your superiors expect you to speak up," I said. "It's not about challenging authority – it's about showing that you're engaged and invested in the outcome."

Gradually, Rohan started communicating more openly with his superiors. He asked questions, shared his insights, and provided feedback. This new approach helped him gain **valuable advice** from his leaders and build stronger professional relationships based on mutual respect.

Presenting Yourself Professionally

Finally, Rohan learned that professionalism goes beyond delivering good work—it's about how you **present yourself.** One day, before a virtual meeting with senior clients in Norway, we talked about the importance of both attire and virtual presence. I told him, "It's not just about what you say—it's how you show up."

At the next meeting, Rohan wore a **sharp blazer and a crisp white shirt,** with a clean, organized background. He also made sure to pace his words carefully, ensuring that everyone *understood him clearly. This attention to detail made an immediate impact—his colleagues in Norway noticed the change, and his credibility soared. Rohan learned that **presentation matters**, and the way you show up can make all the difference in how others perceive you.*

*Rohan's transformation wasn't the result of a single lesson, nor was it something I can take credit for. His success was shaped by his own **dedication, intelligence, and hard work**. He took the advice I shared, but it was Rohan who did the heavy lifting. It was **his** perseverance, punctuality, and relentless drive that allowed him to excel. What I provided were just tools to help him navigate the cultural differences, but it was **Rohan's adoption** that made all the difference.*

Throughout this journey, Rohan didn't lose his identity—he expanded it. He adapted to Western business culture without ever compromising who he was at his core. By learning to bridge cultural differences, he allowed his true talents to be recognized by his Western colleagues, showcasing his brilliance in ways that may not have been fully visible before.

*His hard work and great feedback across the firm didn't go unnoticed. Rohan's hard work earned him one of the most prestigious honors in his firm—the **Presidential Bonus**, an award given to a few out of hundreds of employees.*

The Journey Ahead

As you embark on this journey of mastering the skills outlined in this book, remember that every challenge you overcome is another step toward building the future you deserve. The ability to **navigate cultural nuances, communicate with clarity,** and **build meaningful relationships across borders** is more than just a skill set—it's your competitive edge. In an ever-globalizing world, these abilities will not only differentiate you, but they will also **position you as a leader,** ready to thrive in the workplace of tomorrow.

But this journey isn't just about professional success—it's about personal growth. **Adapting doesn't mean changing who you are; it means becoming the most effective version of yourself.** Every moment you invest in learning these skills will compound over time, creating a ripple effect that touches every aspect of your life and career. These lessons are more than just tools—they are keys to unlocking a future where your contributions will be **recognized, valued, and indispensable.**

The world is becoming smaller, but the opportunities are expanding. In the workplace of tomorrow, those who can bridge cultures with **grace, empathy, and understanding** will be the ones who lead the way. You now hold the skills for success in your hands—but it's your actions that will determine where this journey takes you.

Start today. Master these skills, take control of your path, and remember that your greatest strengths lie in your ability to adapt, learn, and connect. The future is yours to shape, and the possibilities are limitless. **The time to act is now.**

Lars Kåre Helgesen

References

ↀ✼ↀ

The books and sources listed here have been instrumental in shaping *Become the Global Indian*. They provided valuable insights, frameworks, and examples that have influenced the ideas and strategies presented throughout this book. While this is not an exhaustive bibliography, these works represent a curated selection of essential readings that have significantly enriched my understanding of cross-cultural communication, leadership, time management, and trust-building.

If you found the concepts in this book valuable, I highly recommend exploring the works referenced here. They offer deeper perspectives and actionable advice that can further your journey in mastering the nine essential skills for working with the West.

Cross-Cultural Communication

1. Meyer, Erin. *The Culture Map: Breaking Through the Invisible Boundaries of Global Business*. PublicAffairs, 2014.

2. Storti, Craig. *Speaking of India: Bridging the Communication Gap When Working with Indians*. Nicholas Brealey Publishing, 2015.

3. Storti, Craig. *The Art of Crossing Cultures*. 3rd ed., Nicholas Brealey Publishing, 2021.

4. Lewis, Richard D. *When Cultures Collide: Leading Across Cultures*. Nicholas Brealey Publishing, 2018.

Professional Skills

1. Rackham, Neil. *SPIN Selling*. McGraw-Hill Education, 1995.

2. McGowan, Bill. *Pitch Perfect: How to Say It Right the First Time, Every Time*. Harper Business, 2014.

3. Pink, Daniel H. *To Sell Is Human: The Surprising Truth About Moving Others*. Riverhead Books, 2012.

4. Dixon, Matthew, and Adamson, Brent. *The Challenger Sale: Taking Control of the Customer Conversation*. Portfolio, 2011.

Cultural Insights into India

1. Sen, Amartya. *The Argumentative Indian: Writings on Indian History, Culture, and Identity*. Farrar, Straus and Giroux, 2005.

2. Das, Gurcharan. *India Unbound: The Social and Economic Revolution from Independence to the Global Information Age*. Anchor Books, 2002.

3. Tharoor, Shashi. *Inglorious Empire: What the British Did to India*. Hurst Publishers, 2017.

4. Eck, Diana L. *India: A Sacred Geography*. Harmony Books, 2012.

Western Workplace Norms

1. Covey, Stephen R. *The Seven Habits of Highly Effective People: Powerful Lessons in Personal Change*. Free Press, 1989.

2. Fisher, Roger, Ury, William, and Patton, Bruce. *Getting to Yes: Negotiating Agreement Without Giving In*. Penguin Books, 1981.

3. Newport, Cal. *Deep Work: Rules for Focused Success in a Distracted World*. Grand Central Publishing, 2016.

4. Catmull, Ed. *Creativity, Inc.: Overcoming the Unseen Forces That Stand in the Way of True Inspiration*. Random House, 2014.

5. Hyatt, Michael, and Hyatt Miller, Megan. *Win at Work and Succeed at Life: 5 Principles to Free Yourself from the Cult of Overwork*. Baker Books, 2021.

6. Friedman, Thomas L. *The World Is Flat: A Brief History of the Twenty-First Century*. Farrar, Straus and Giroux, 2005.

Building Trust

1. Covey, Stephen M.R. *The Speed of Trust: The One Thing That Changes Everything*. Free Press, 2006.

2. Reina, Dennis S., and Reina, Michelle L. *Trust and Betrayal in the Workplace: Building Effective Relationships in Your Organization*. Berrett-Koehler Publishers, 2006.

3. Feltman, Charles. *The Thin Book of Trust: An Essential Primer for Building Trust at Work*. Thin Book Publishing, 2009.

Persuasion and Communication

1. Heinrichs, Jay. *Thank You for Arguing: What Aristotle, Lincoln, and Homer Simpson Can Teach Us About the Art of Persuasion.* Crown, 2013.

2. Cialdini, Robert B. *Influence: The Psychology of Persuasion.* Harper Business, 2006.

3. Patterson, Kerry, et al. *Crucial Conversations: Tools for Talking When Stakes Are High.* McGraw-Hill Education, 2011.

Leadership and Influence

1. Sinek, Simon. *Leaders Eat Last: Why Some Teams Pull Together and Others Don't.* Portfolio, 2014.

2. Lencioni, Patrick. *The Five Dysfunctions of a Team: A Leadership Fable.* Jossey-Bass, 2002.

3. The Arbinger Institute. *Leadership and Self-Deception: Getting Out of the Box.* Berrett-Koehler Publishers, 2000.

Take Your Learning Further

⁓✳⁓

Congratulations on completing *Become the Global Indian*! You've already taken the first step toward mastering the skills to thrive in Western work environments. Now, it's time to dive deeper and put these skills into action with the **full Global Indian course** available at www.larshelgesen.com.

Here's what you'll get:

- *Exclusive Videos: Watch me walk you through each skill with practical insights and examples.*
- *Engaging Animations: Visualize the key concepts for better understanding and retention.*
- *Scenario-Based Quizzes: Test your knowledge with real-life situations and sharpen your decision-making.*
- *Official Certification: Earn a certificate to showcase your expertise as a Global Indian.*
- **Free Cheat Sheet:** Download a handy guide to the 9 essential skills—perfect for keeping with you at all times.
- *And much more: Additional tools, resources, and guidance to support your journey.*

As a reader of this book and a proud member of the Global Indian community, you can use the code **TGI2025** to get **10% off** the course price.

Start today—visit www.larshelgesen.com and continue your journey toward global success!

About the Author

Lars Kåre Helgesen is a consultant with years of global experience at one of the big four consultancy firms. With a Master's degree in Business and Finance from the Norwegian School of Economics, he has a deep understanding of what it takes to thrive in the competitive Western corporate landscape—knowledge gained not through theory, but from hands-on experience in the field.

What sets him apart is his passion for cross-cultural integration, sparked during his six-month immersion in India, where he worked closely with Indian professionals to break down cultural barriers and bridge gaps in understanding. This led him to develop and deliver courses on cross-cultural collaboration and, eventually, to write *'Become The Global Indian'*, a guide aimed at helping Indian professionals unlock their full potential in the Western workplace.

Driven by the belief that Indian talent is often overlooked due to cultural misunderstandings, Lars is on a mission to change that. His book isn't just about navigating Western business environments – it's about ensuring Indian professionals get the recognition and respect they deserve, armed with the tools to succeed on a global scale.

www.ingramcontent.com/pod-product-compliance
Lightning Source LLC
Chambersburg PA
CBHW021345150726
47989CB00005B/2109